Coloring book for adults and kids beautiful girl image for design

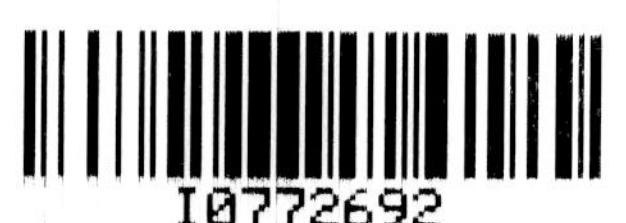

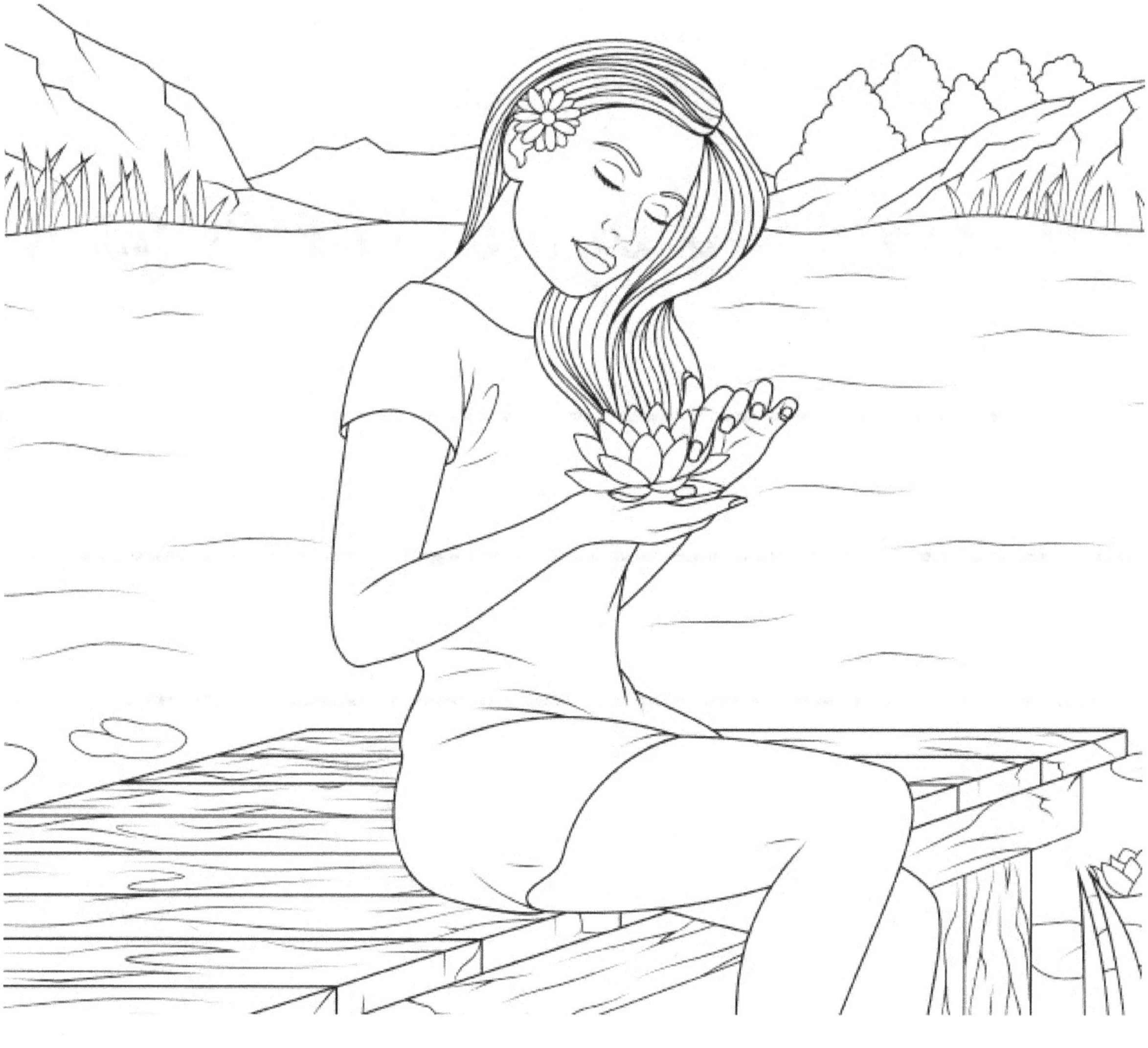

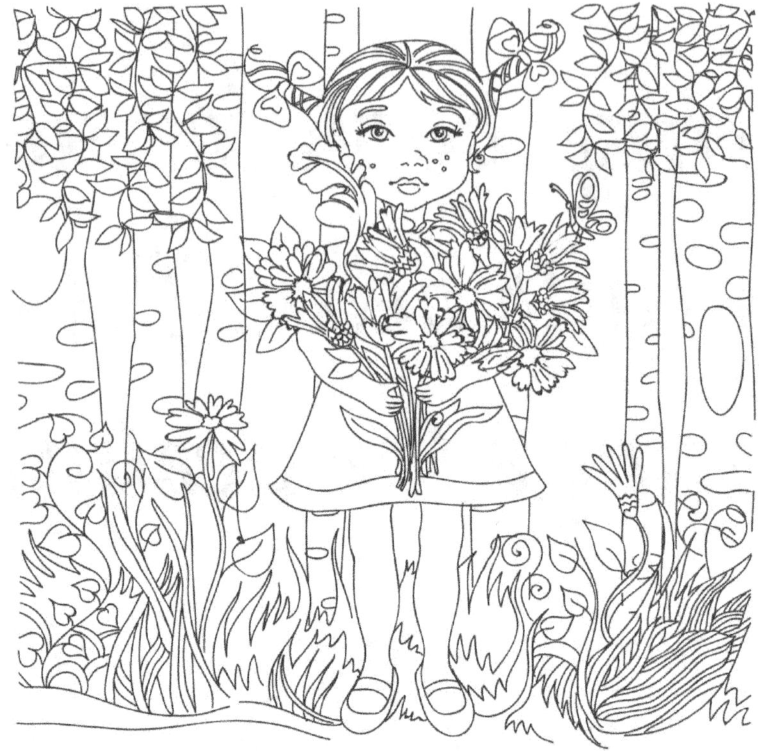

This coloring book is belongs to

____

____

____

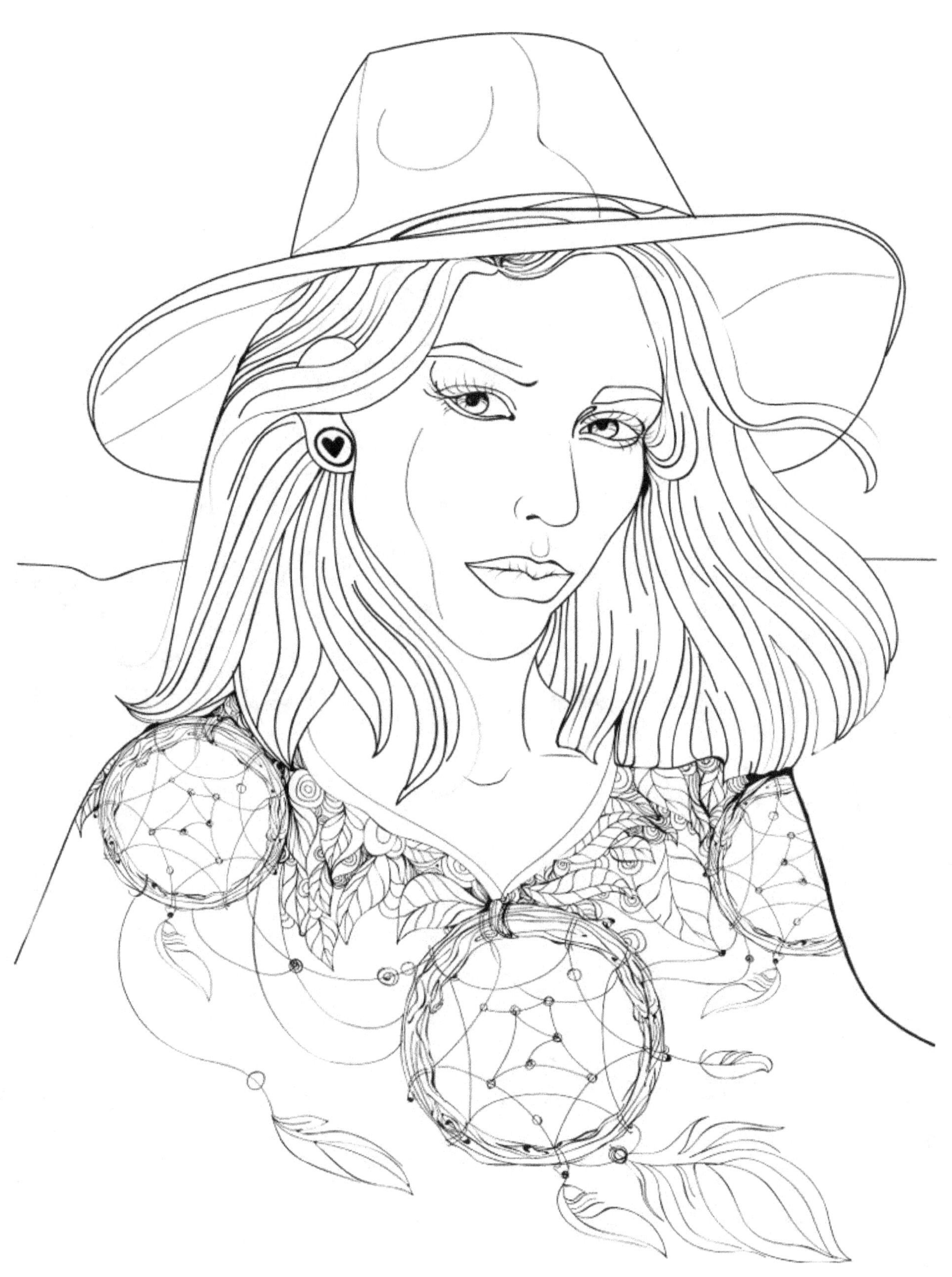

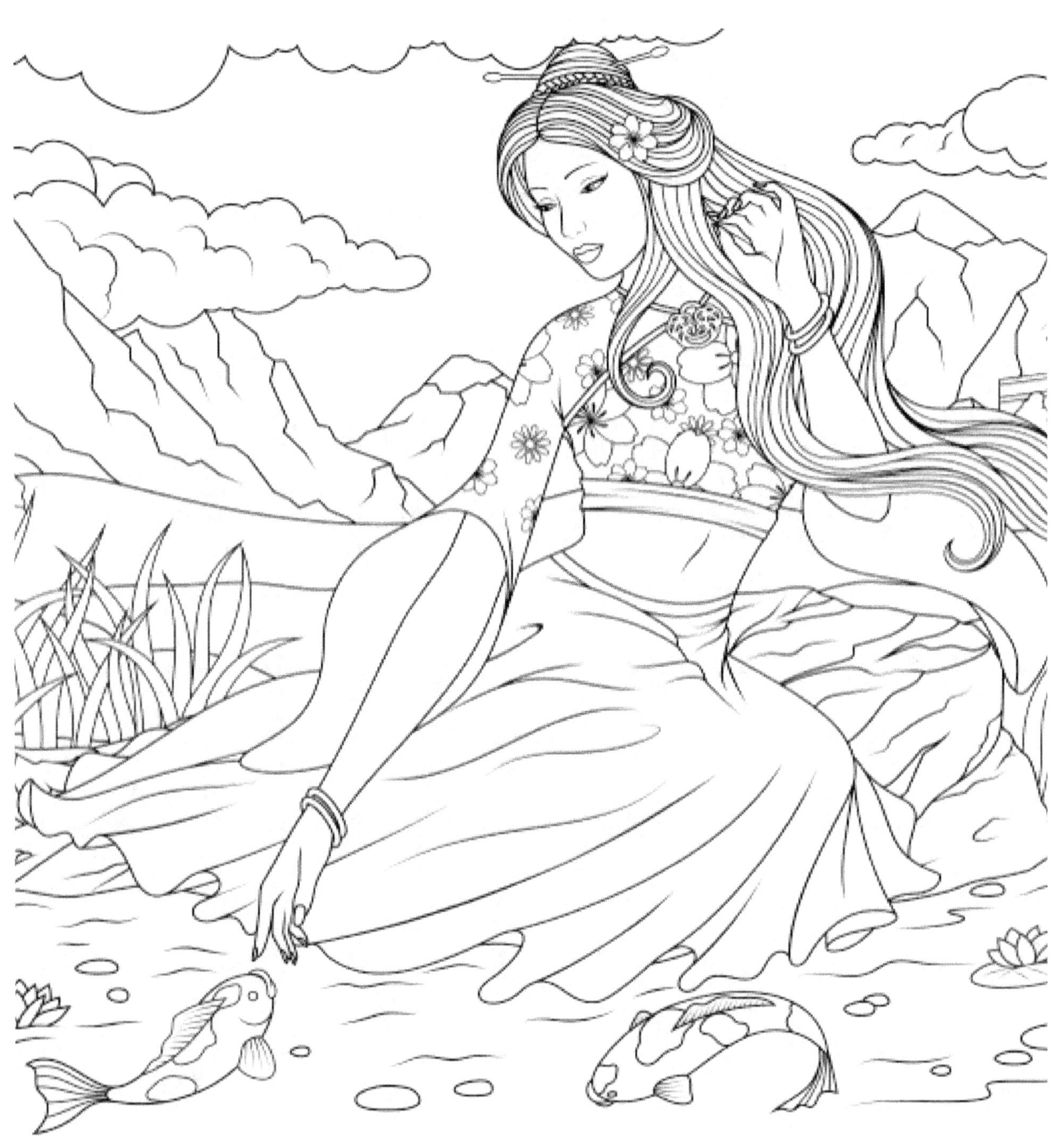

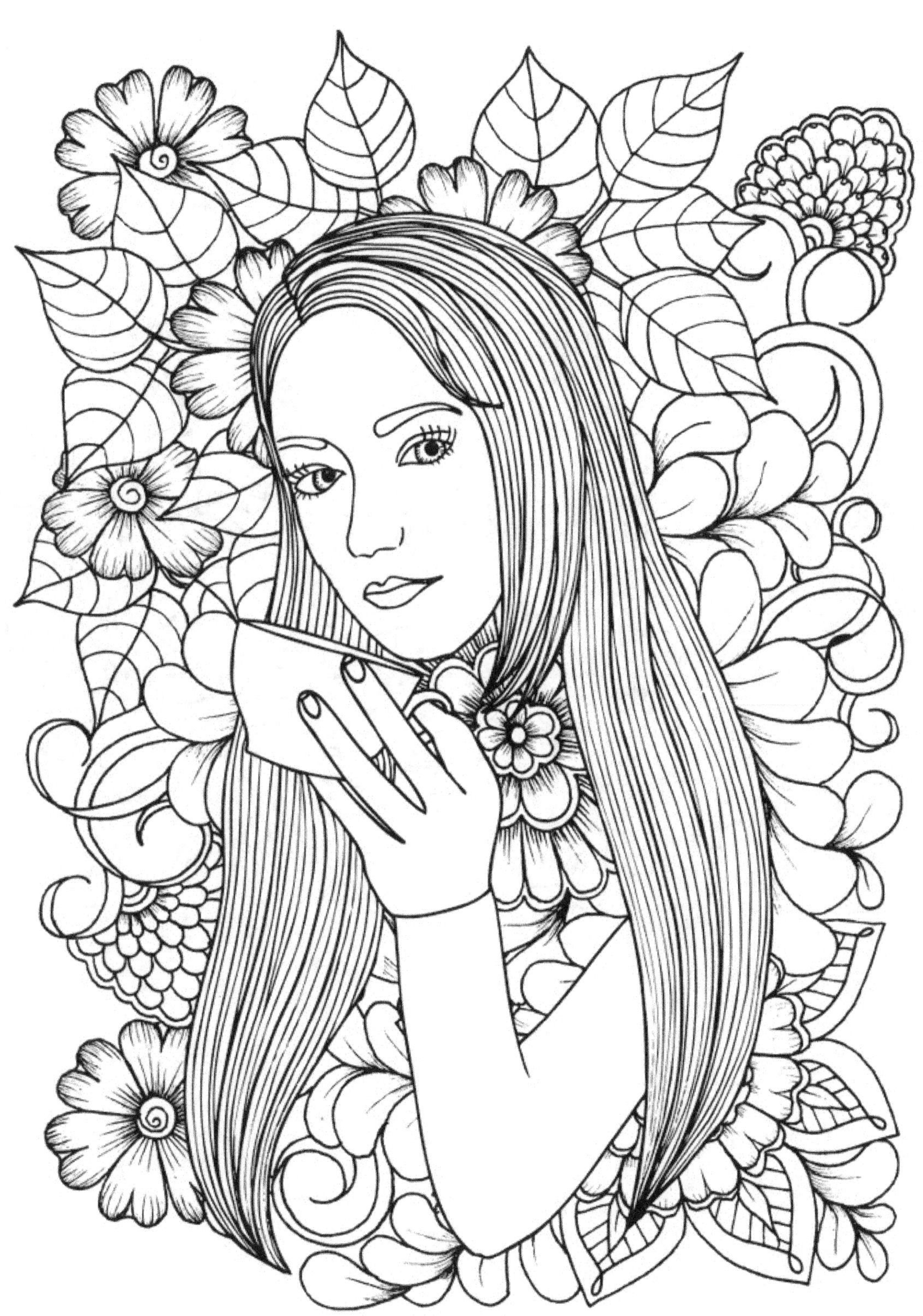

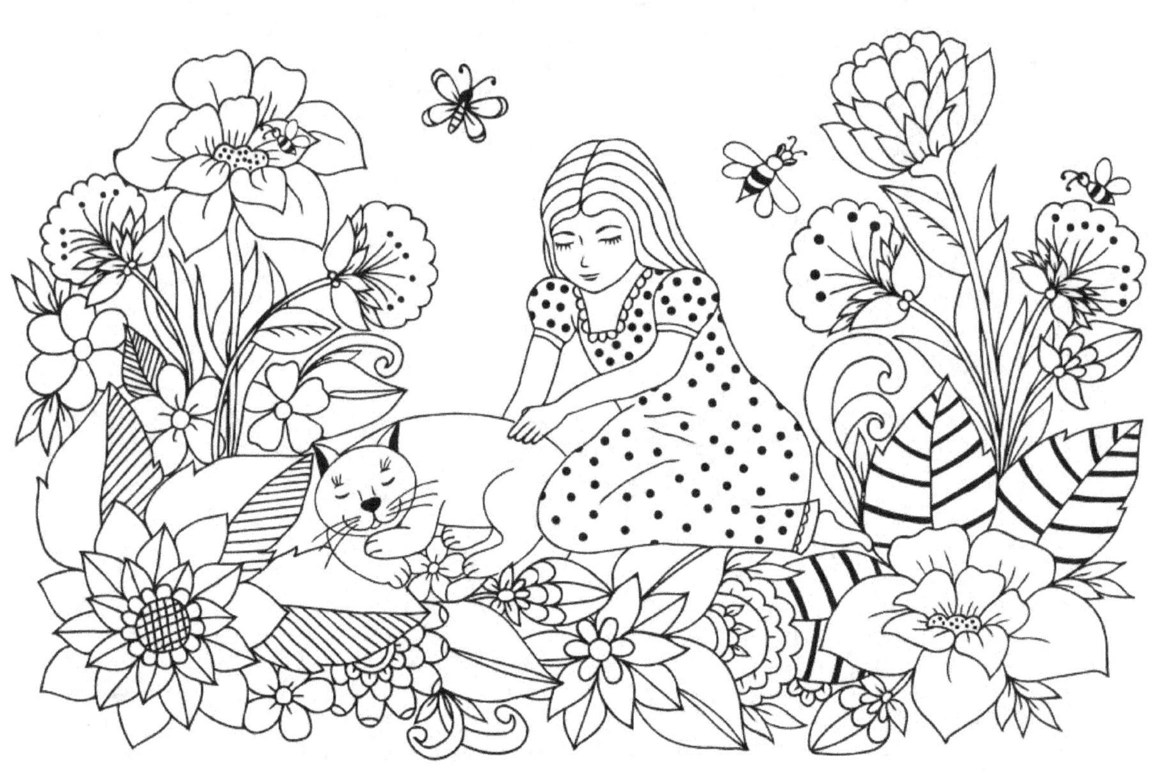

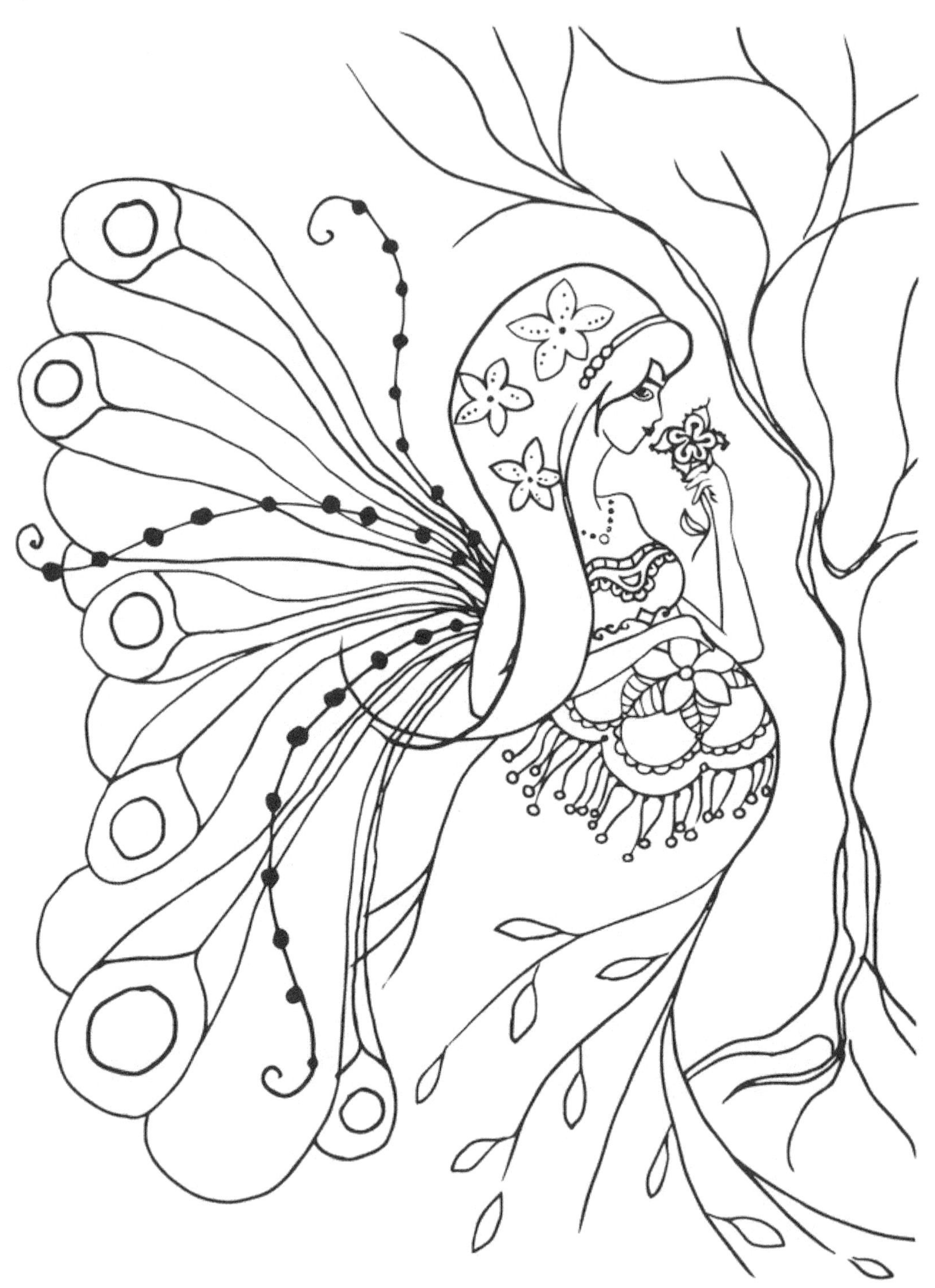

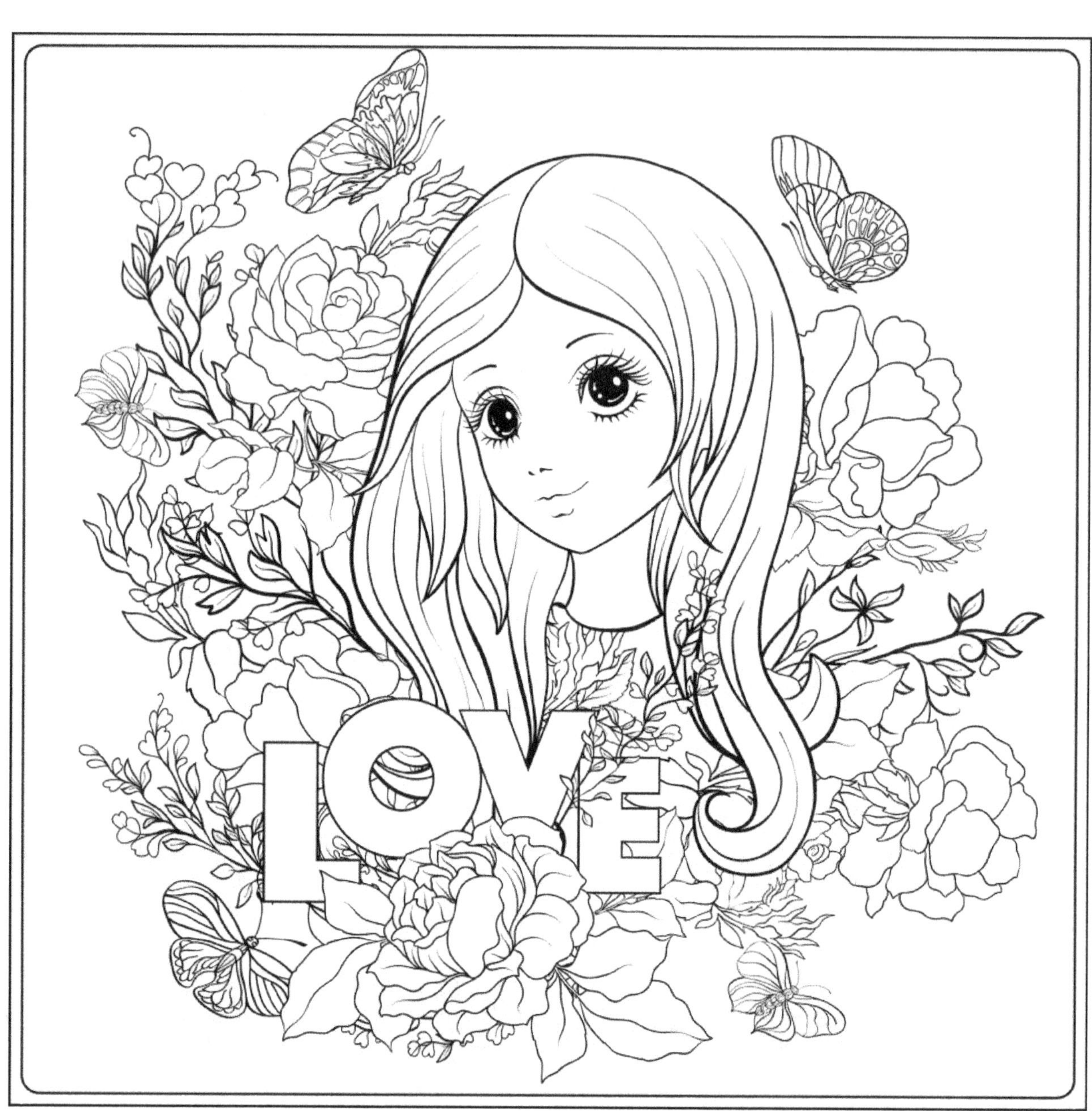
LOVE

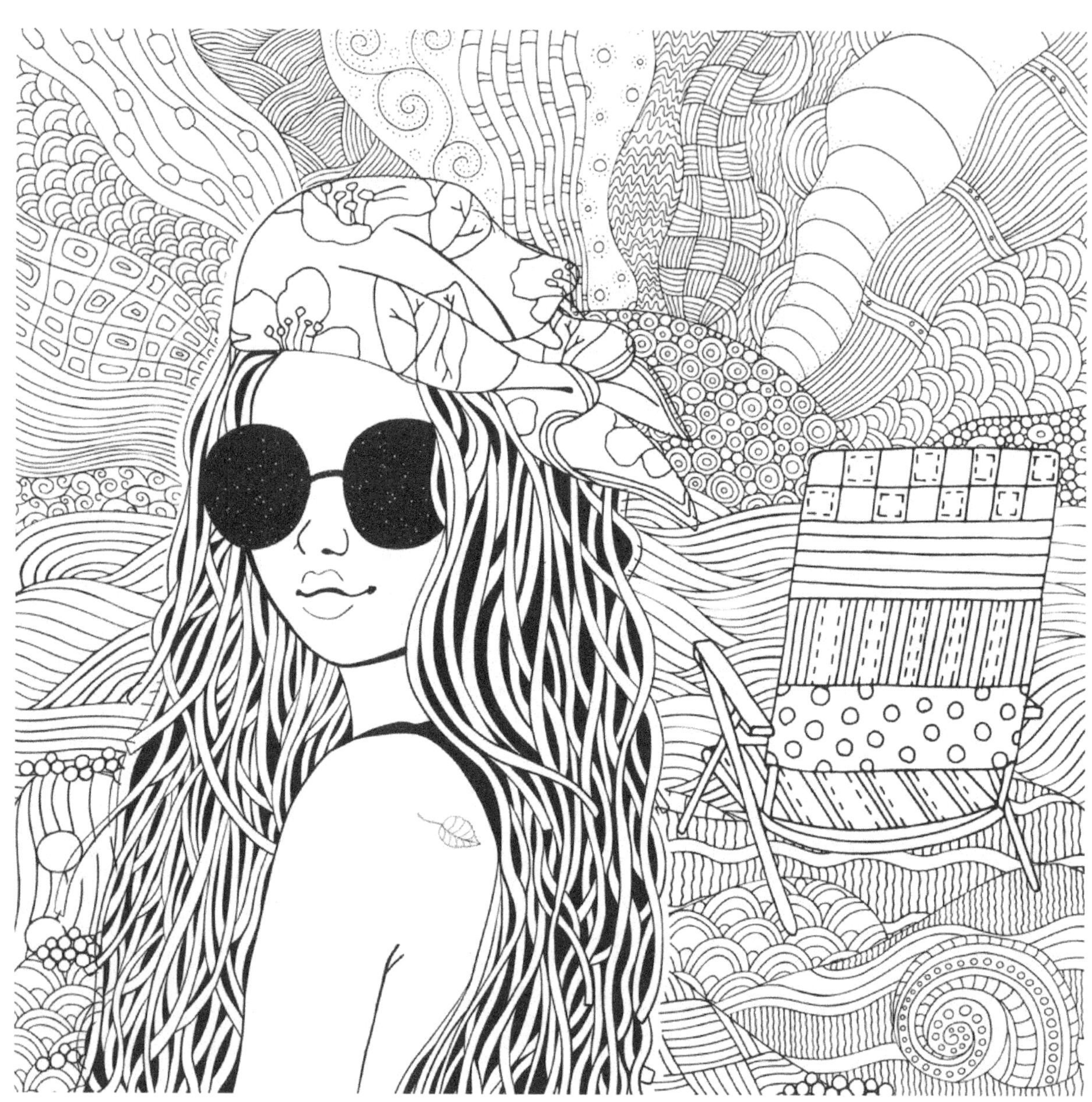

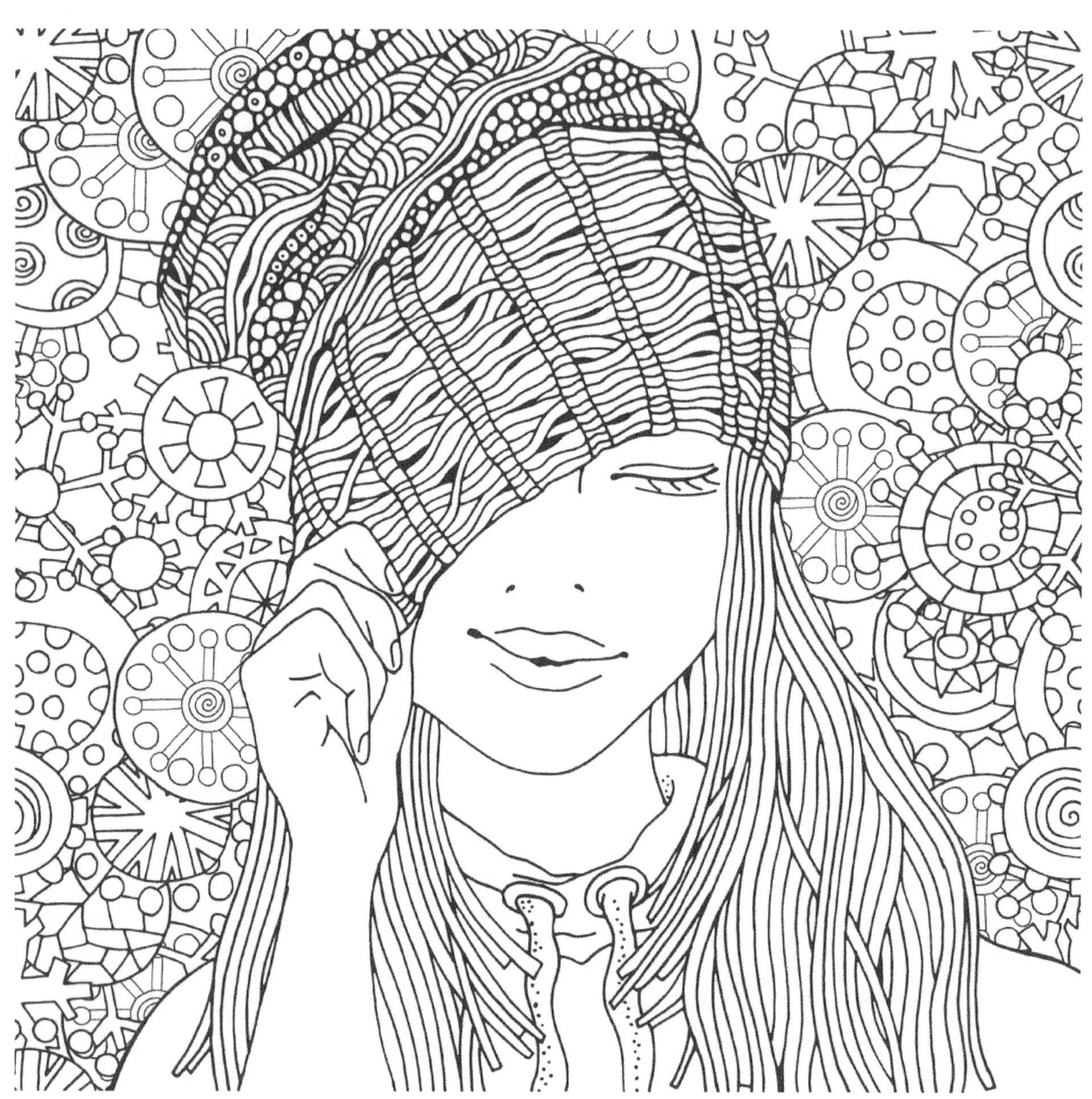

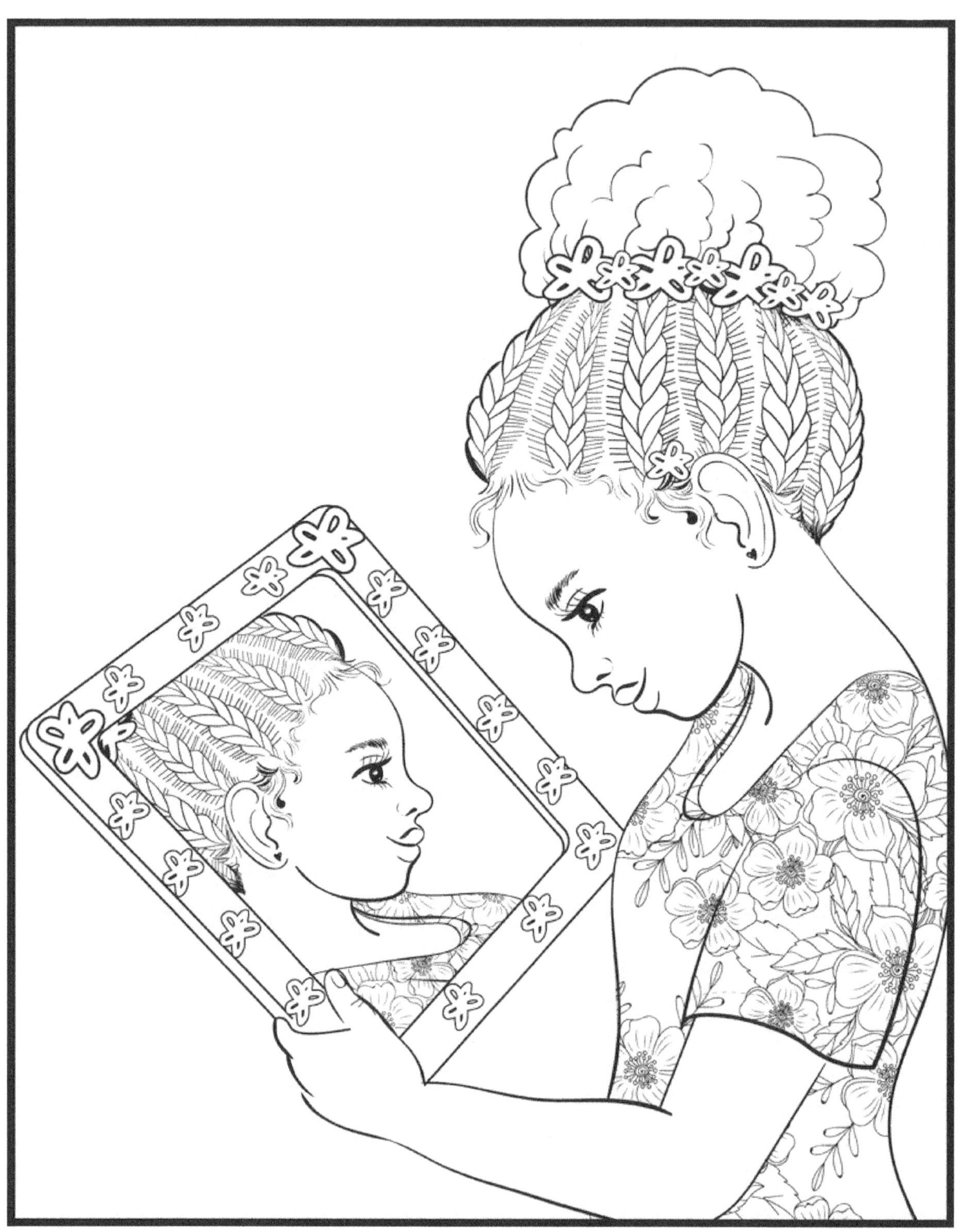

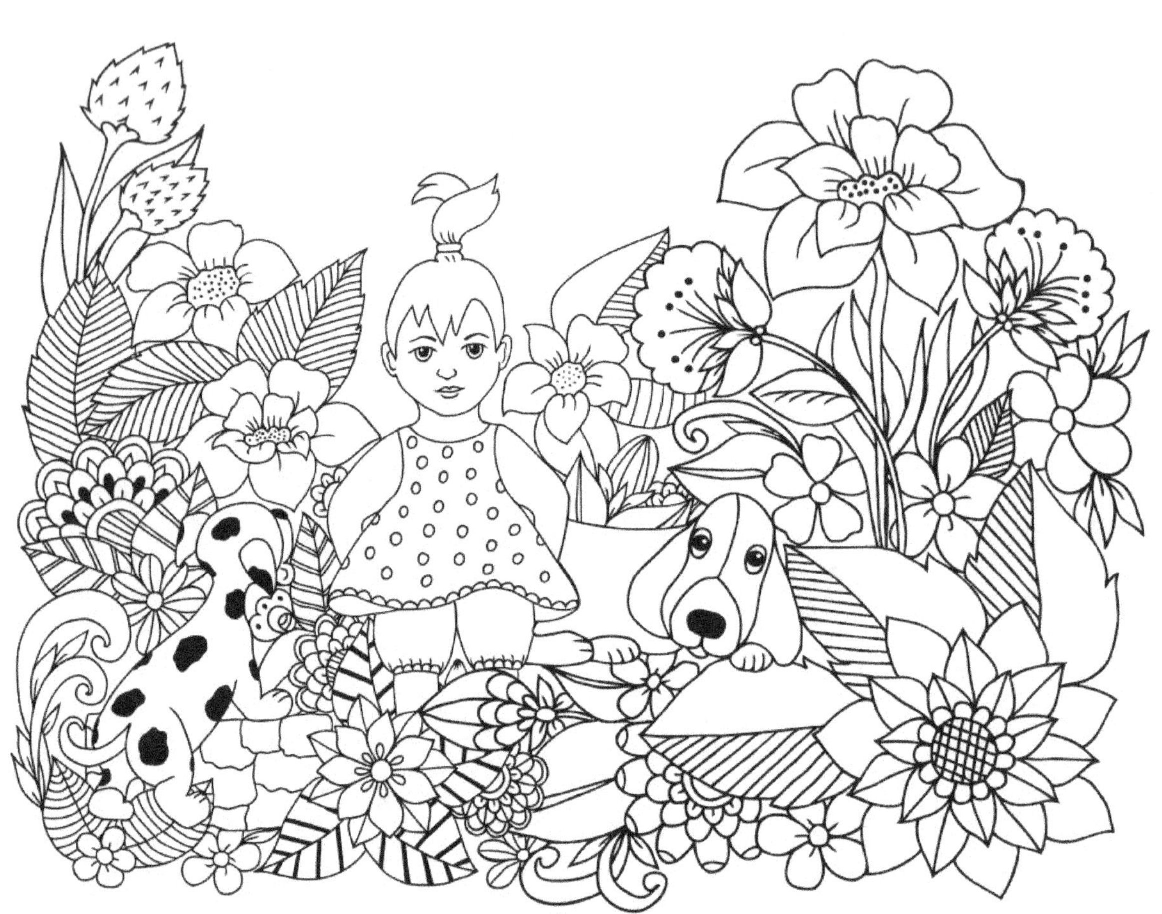

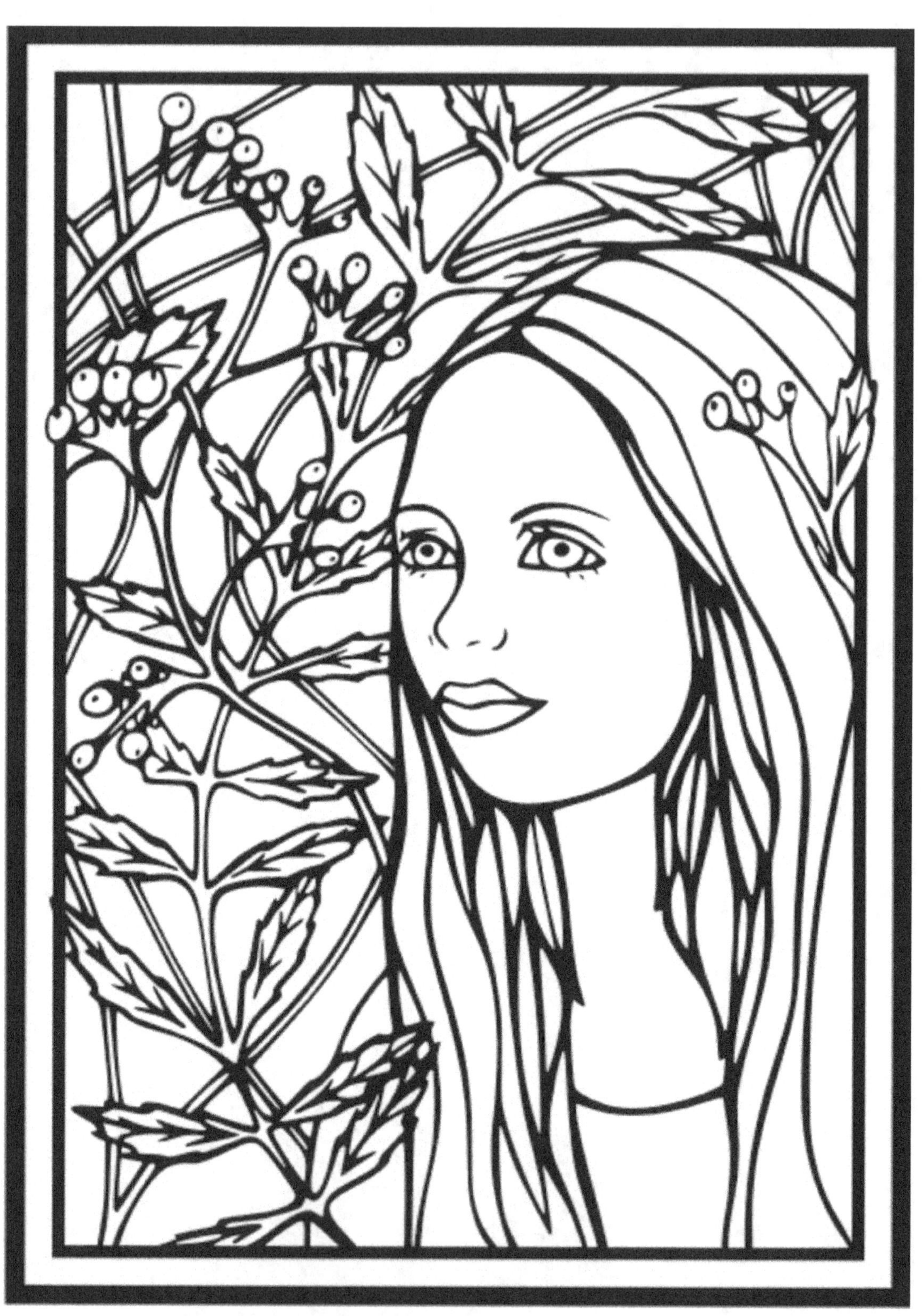

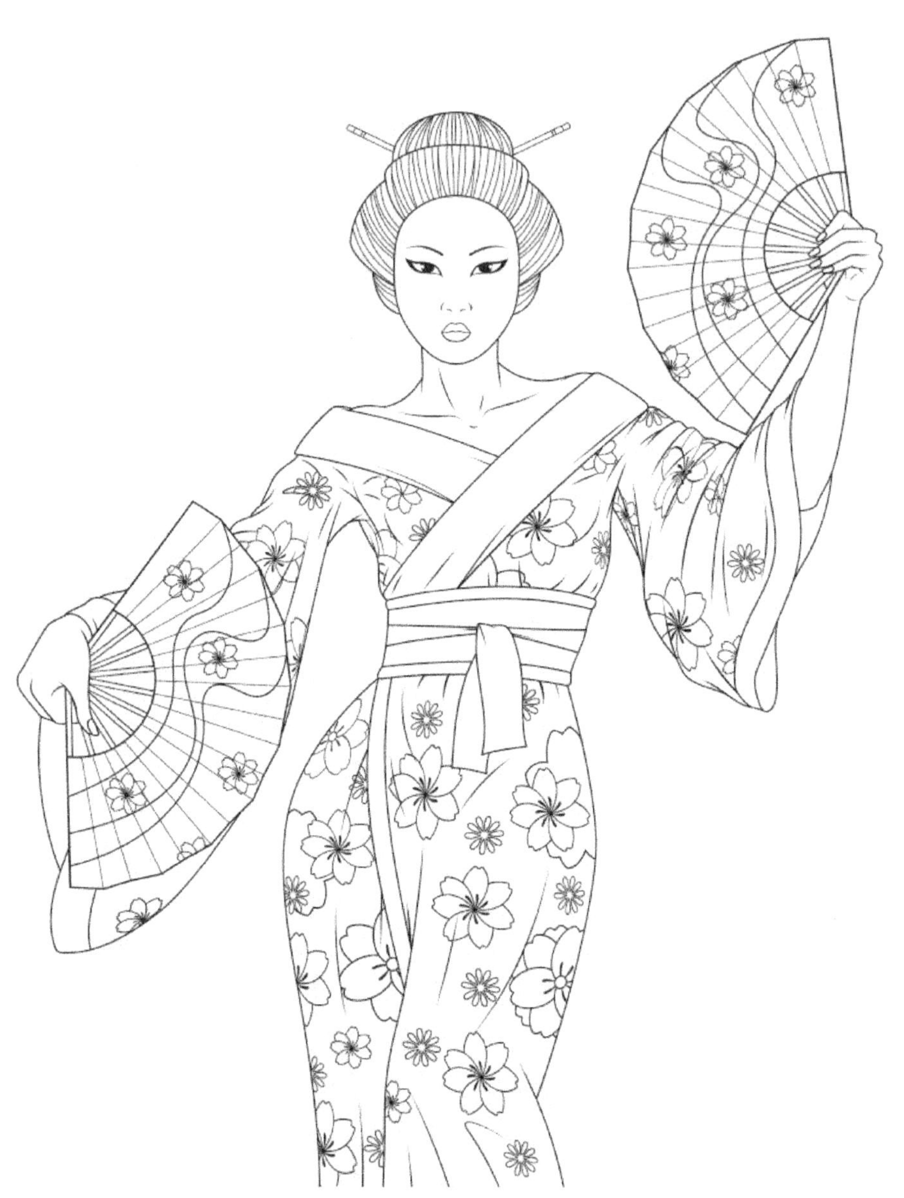

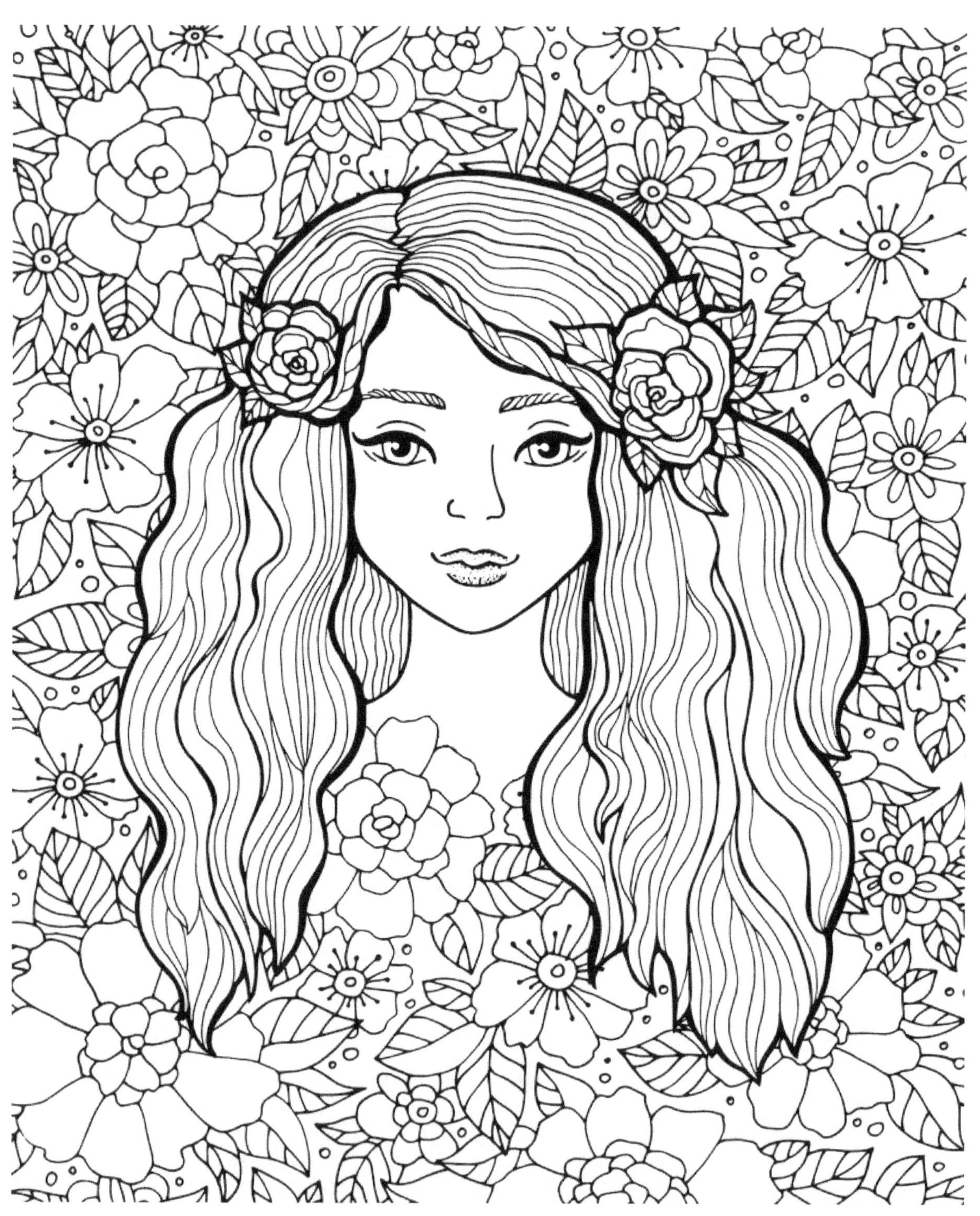

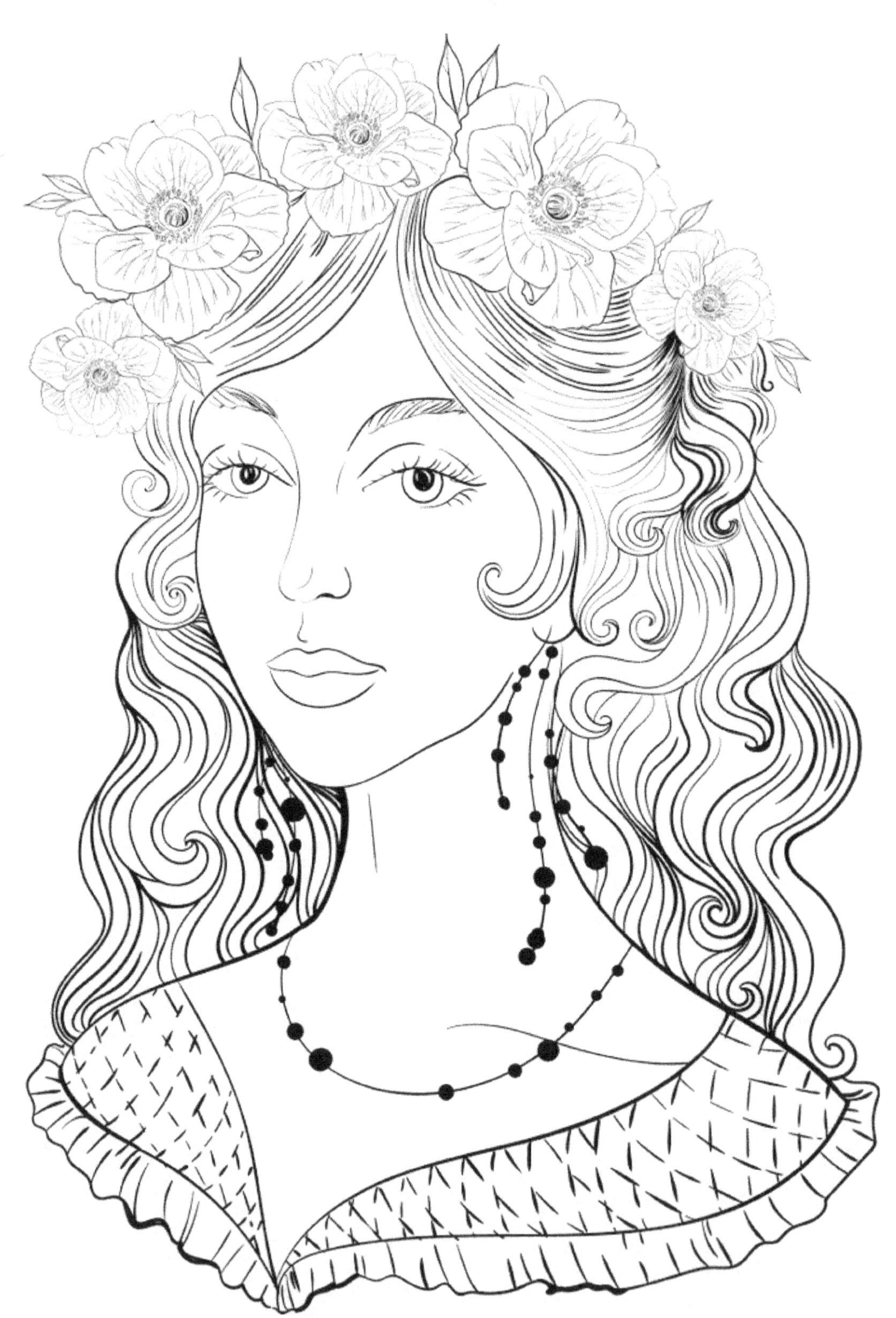

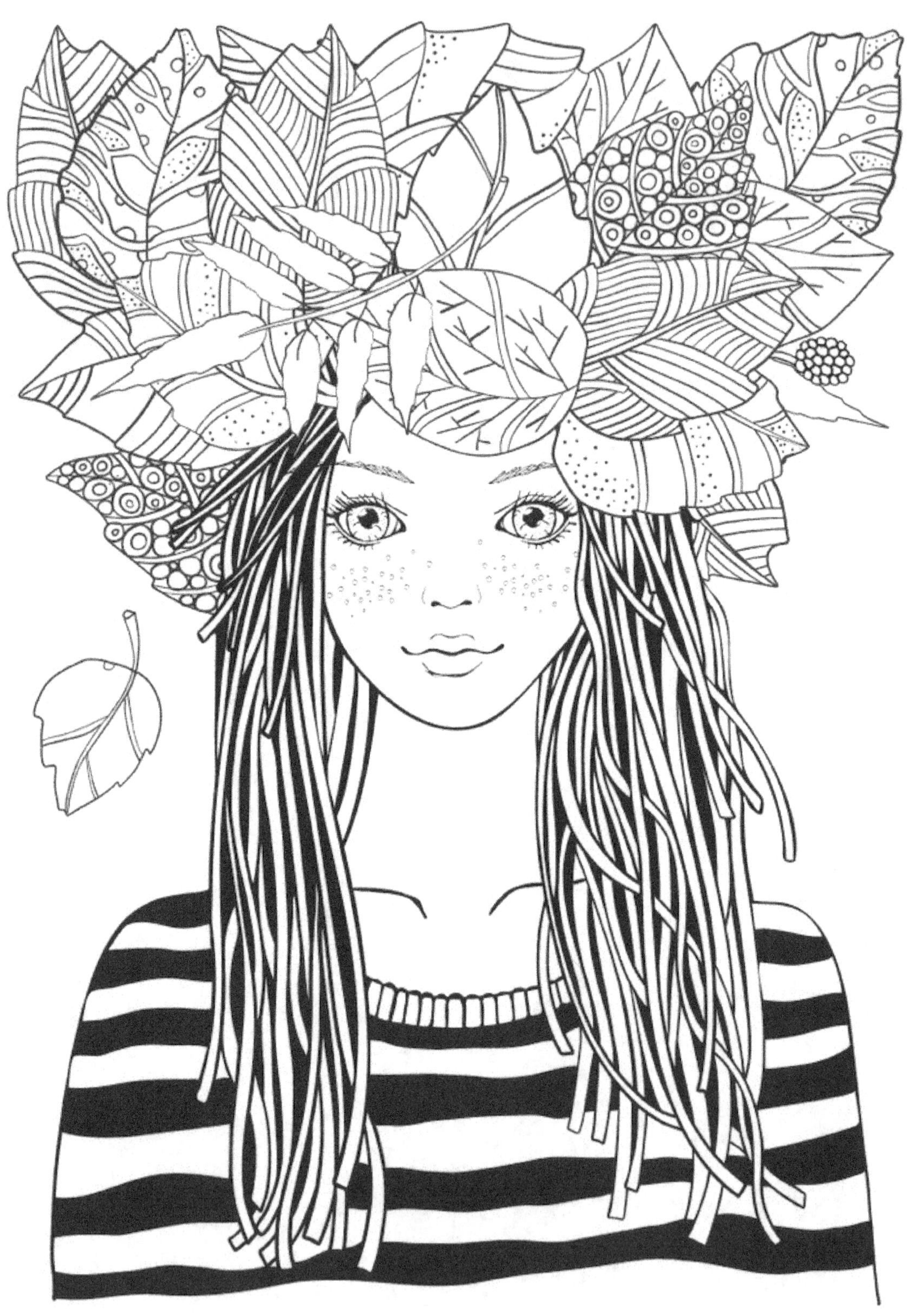

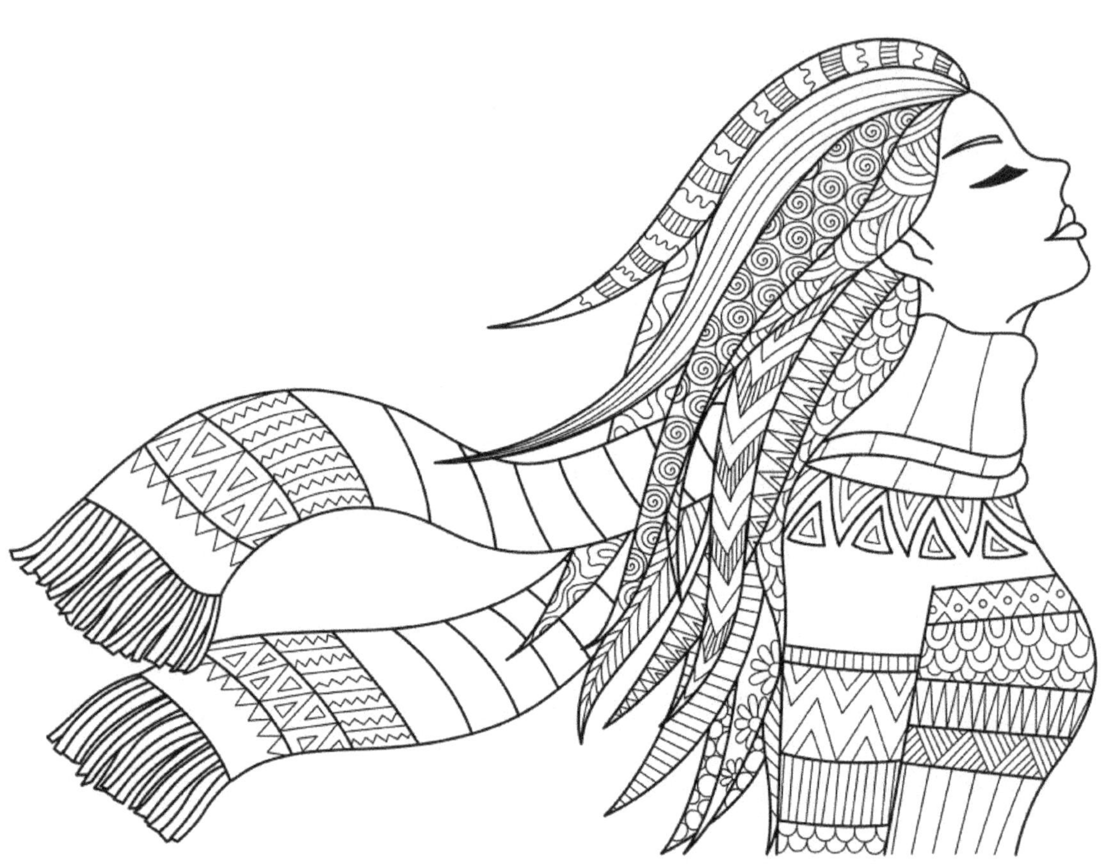

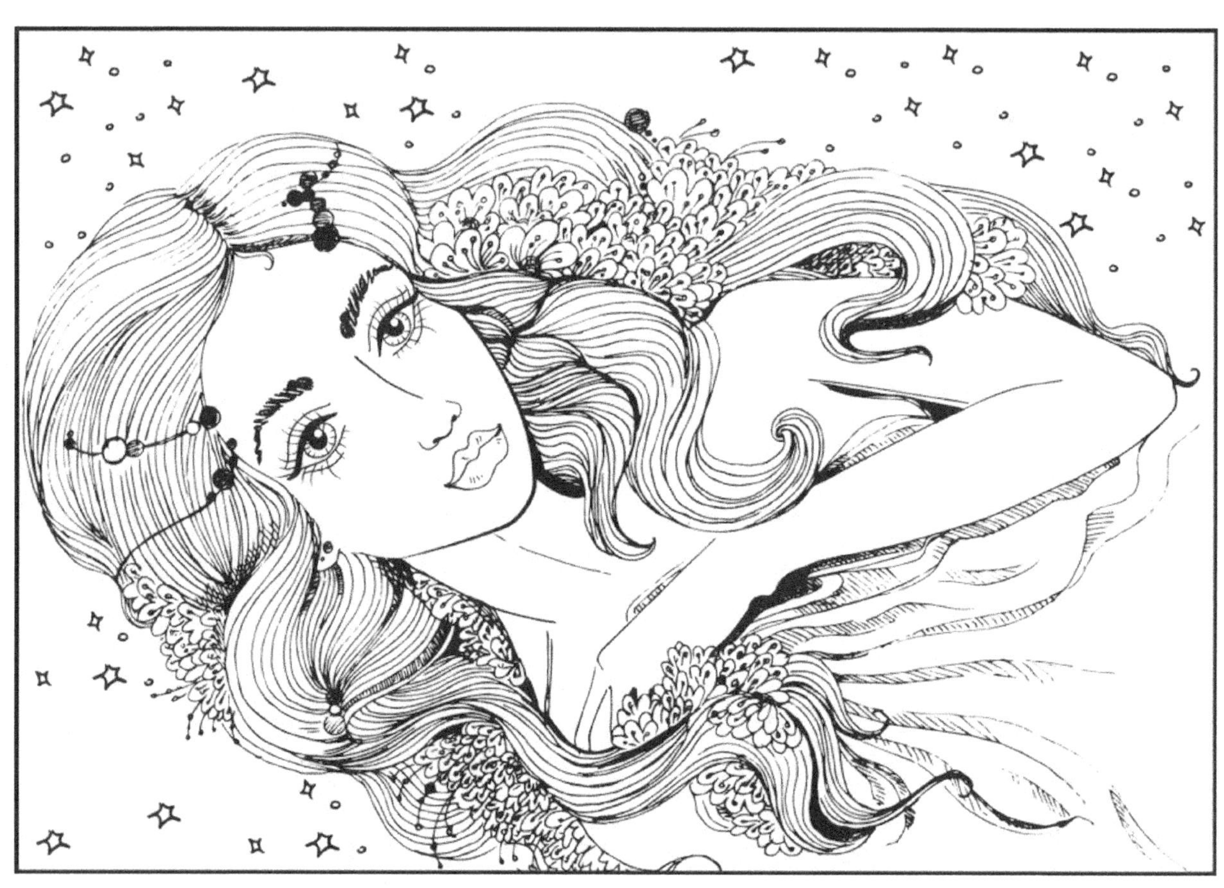

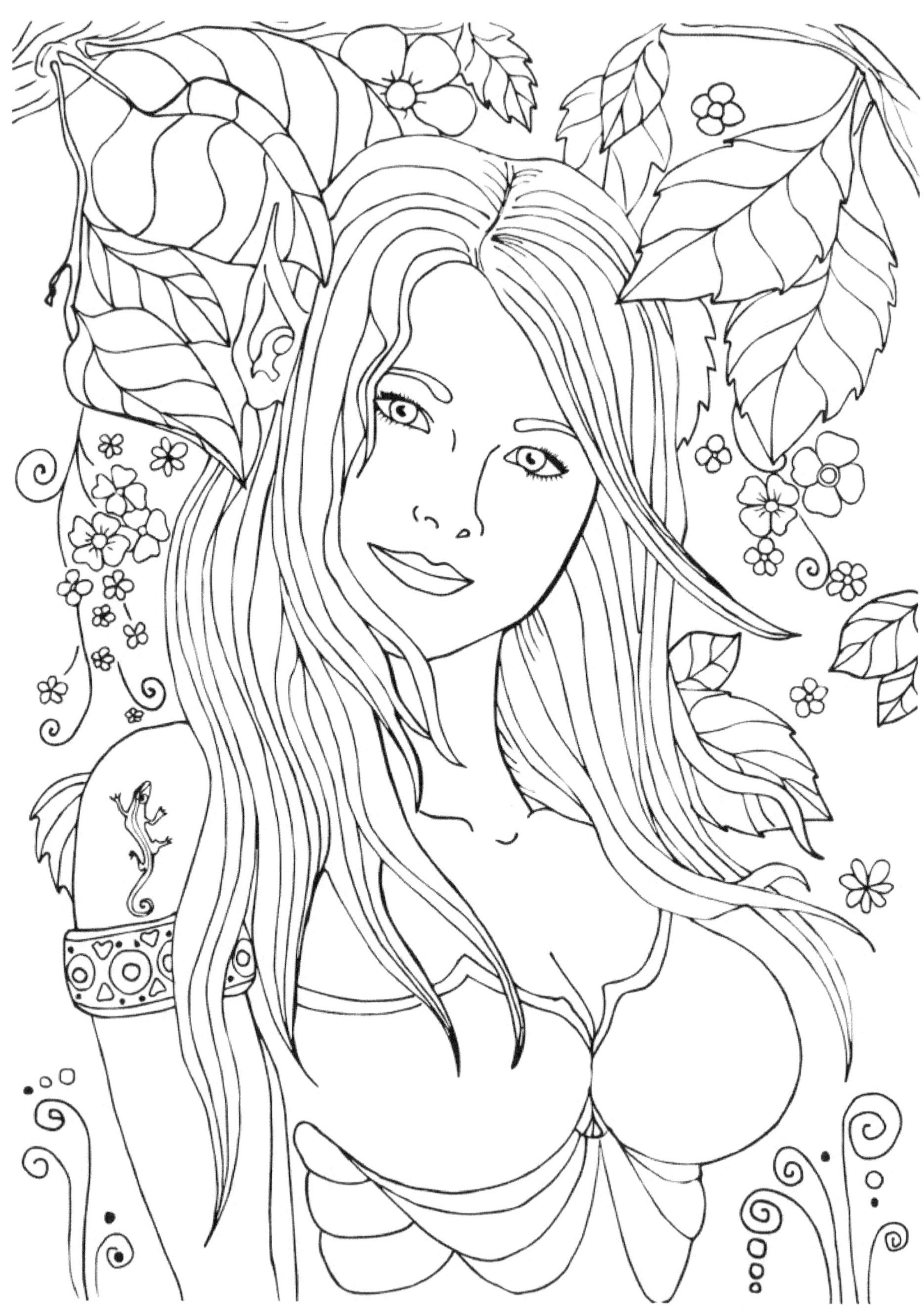

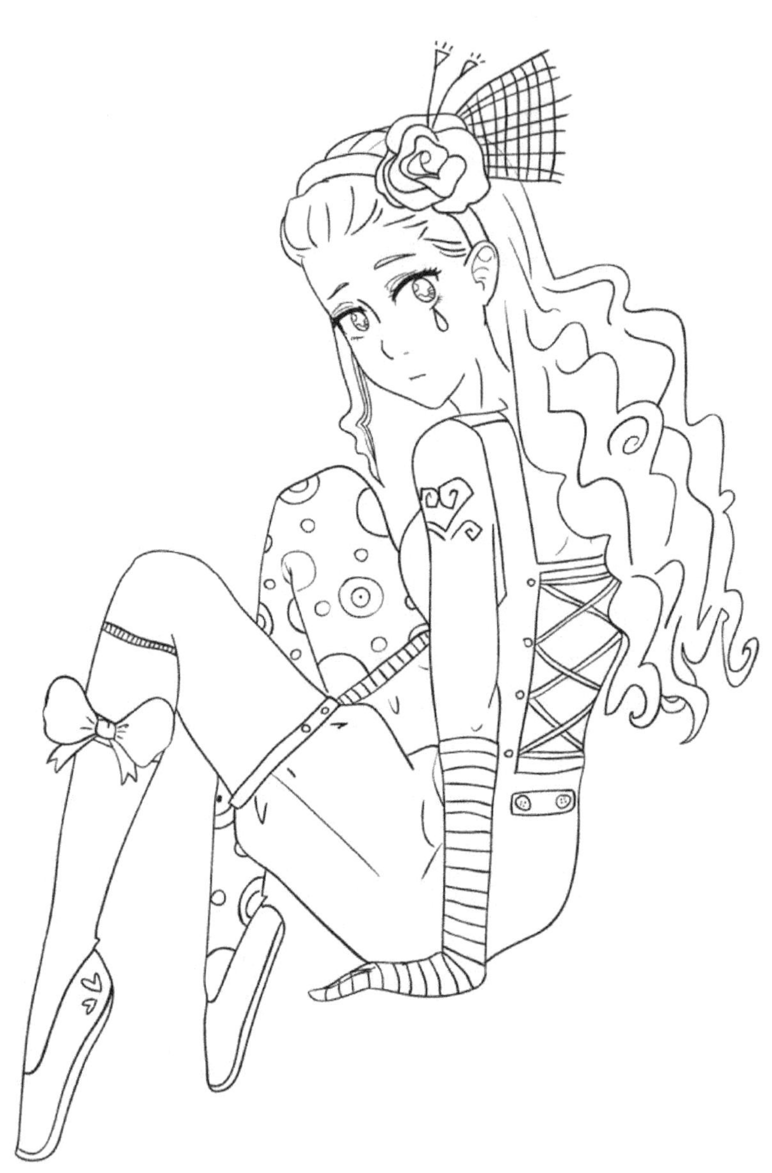

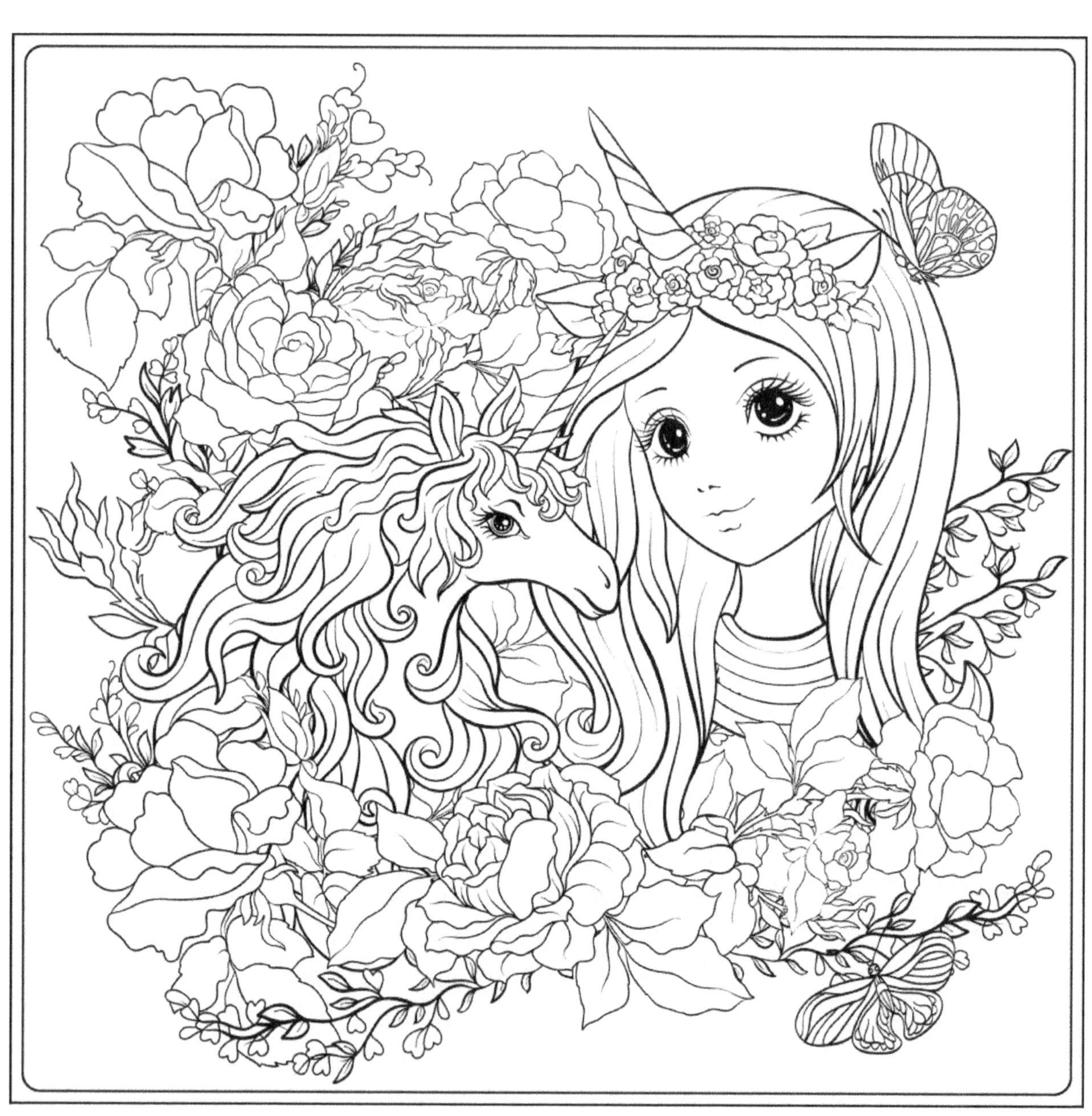

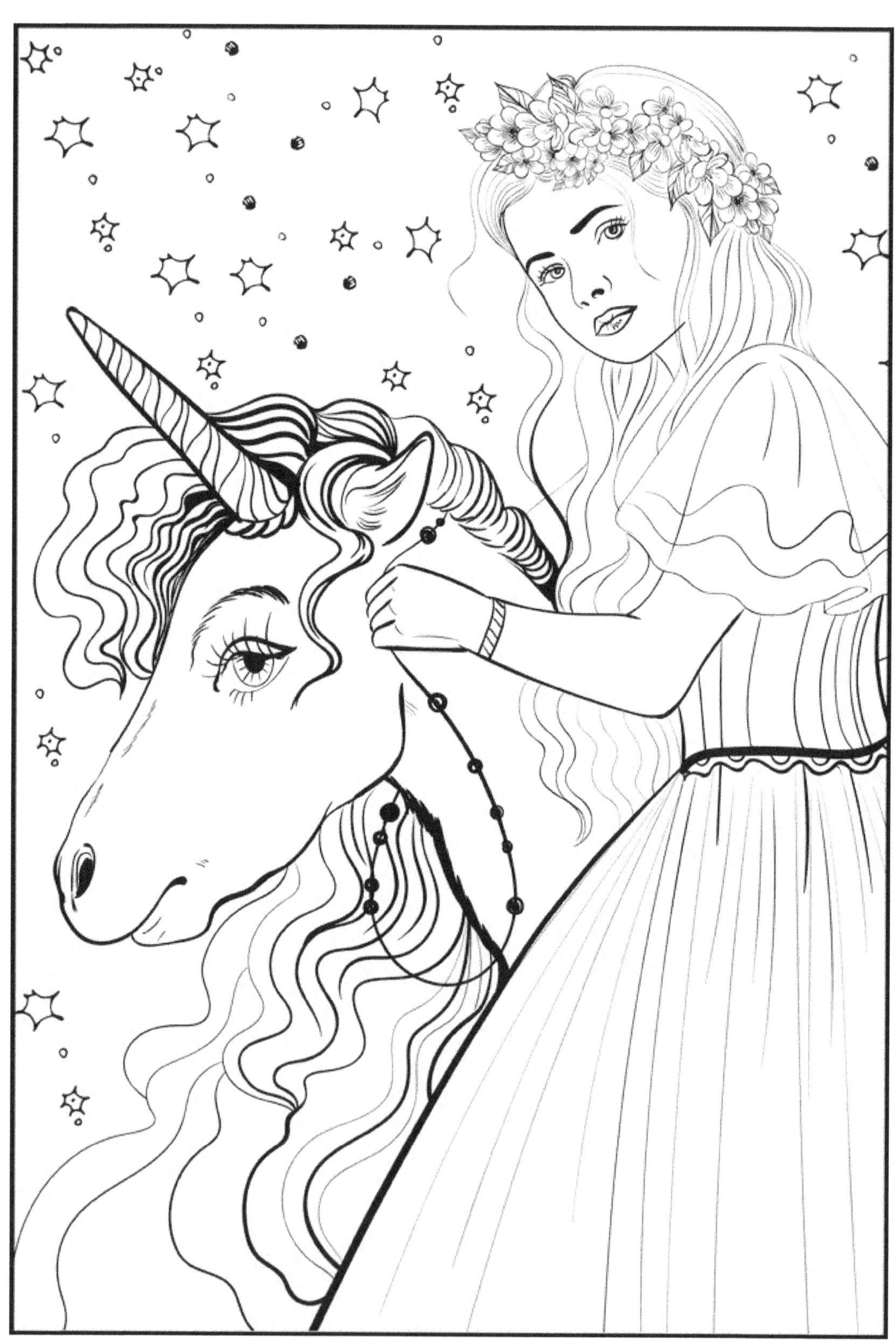

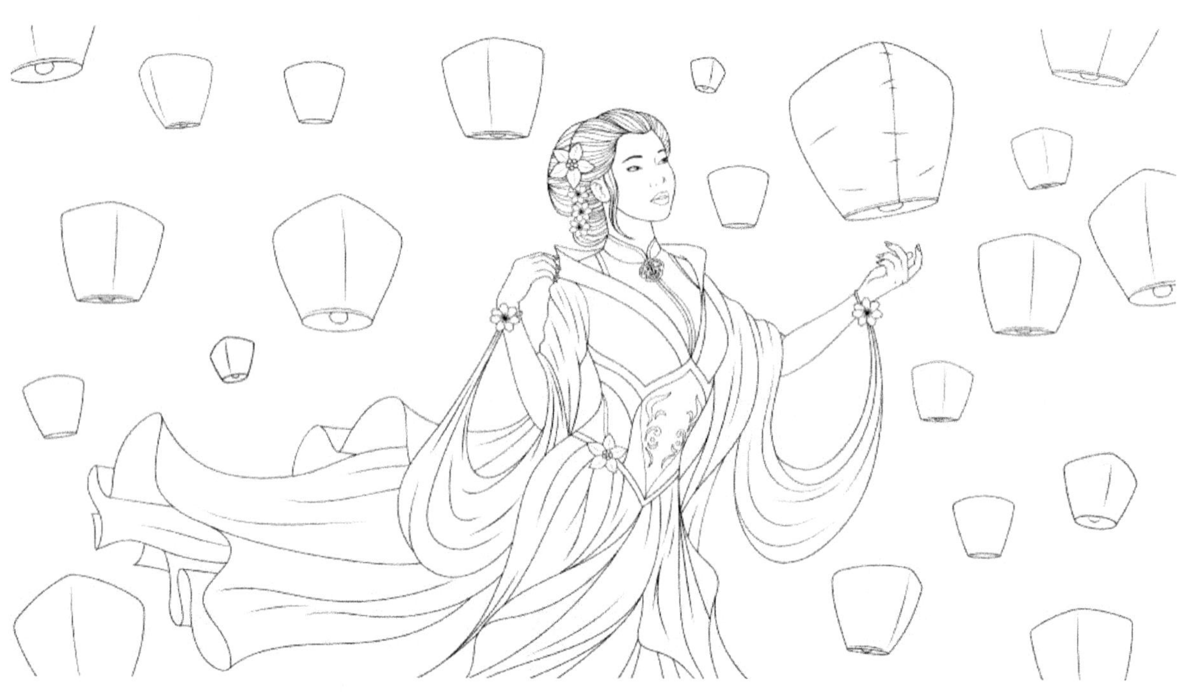

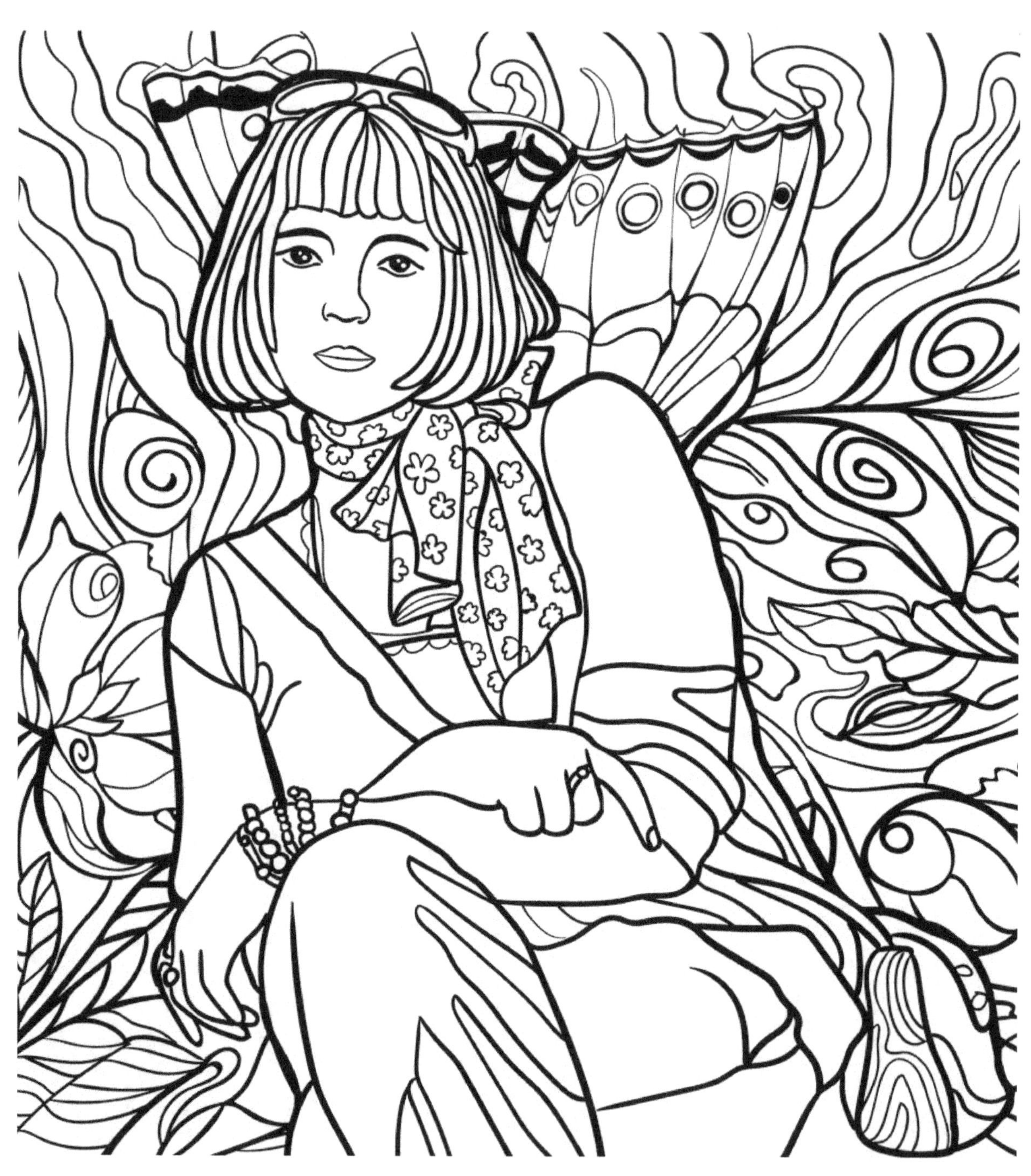

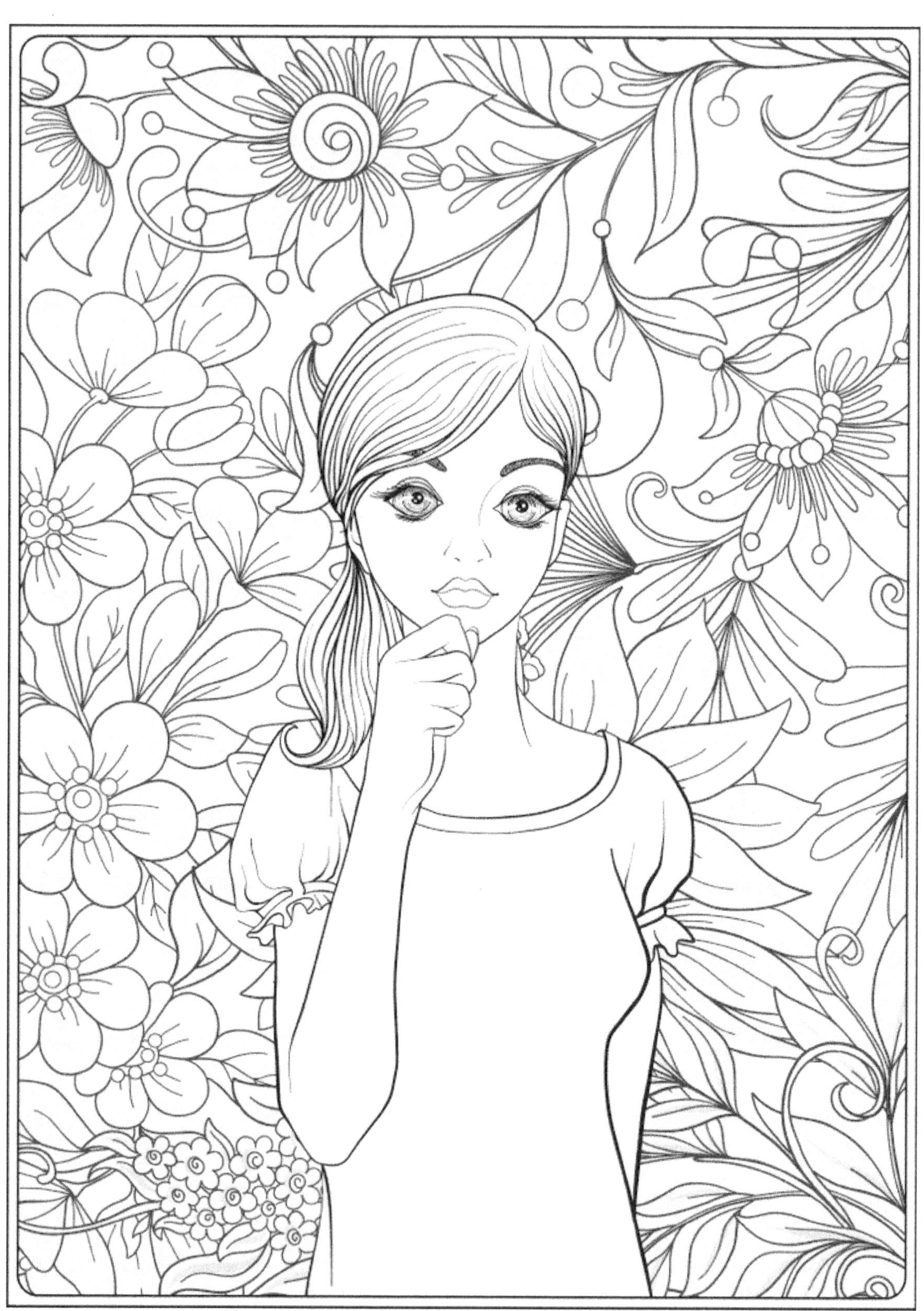

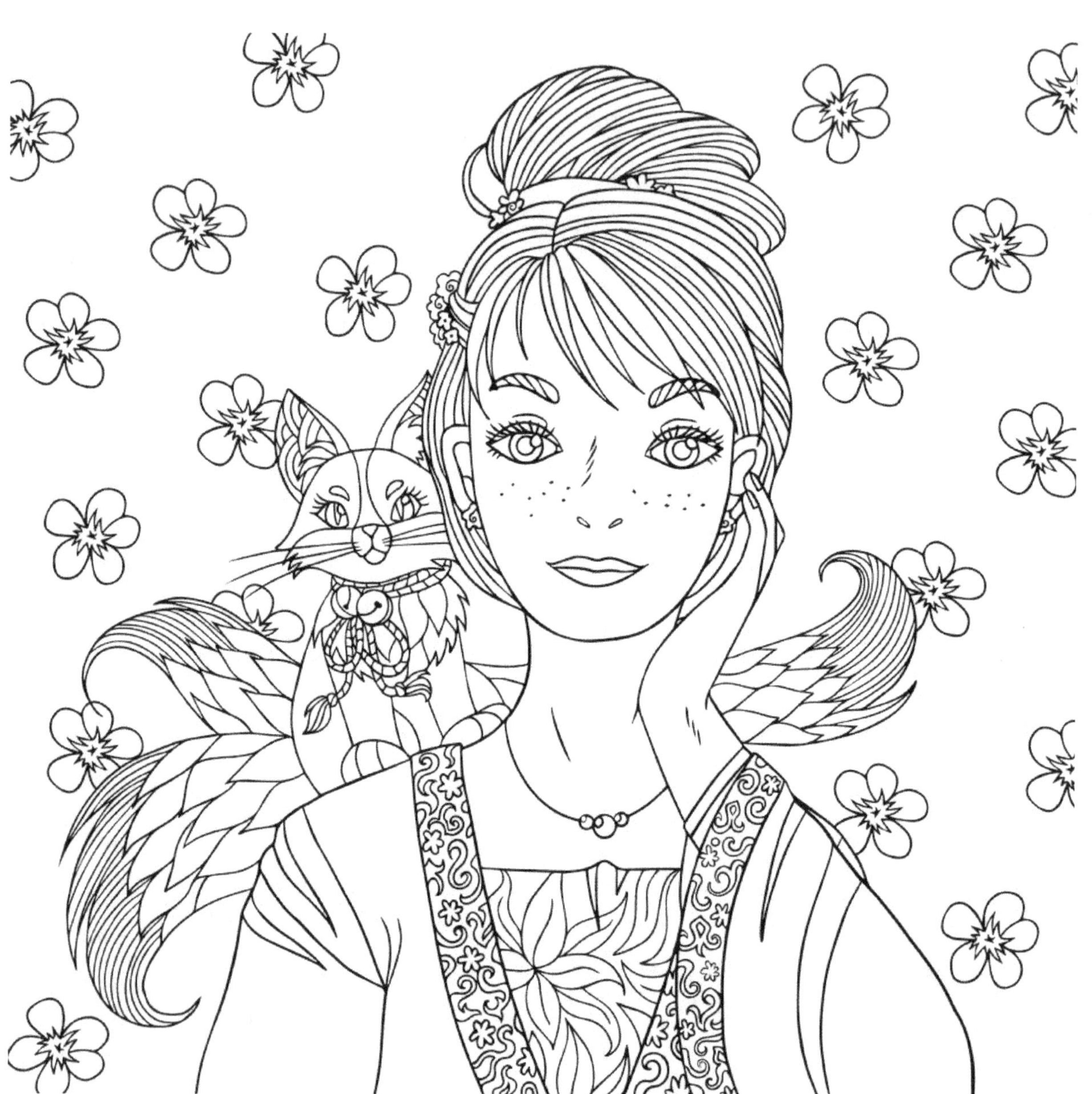

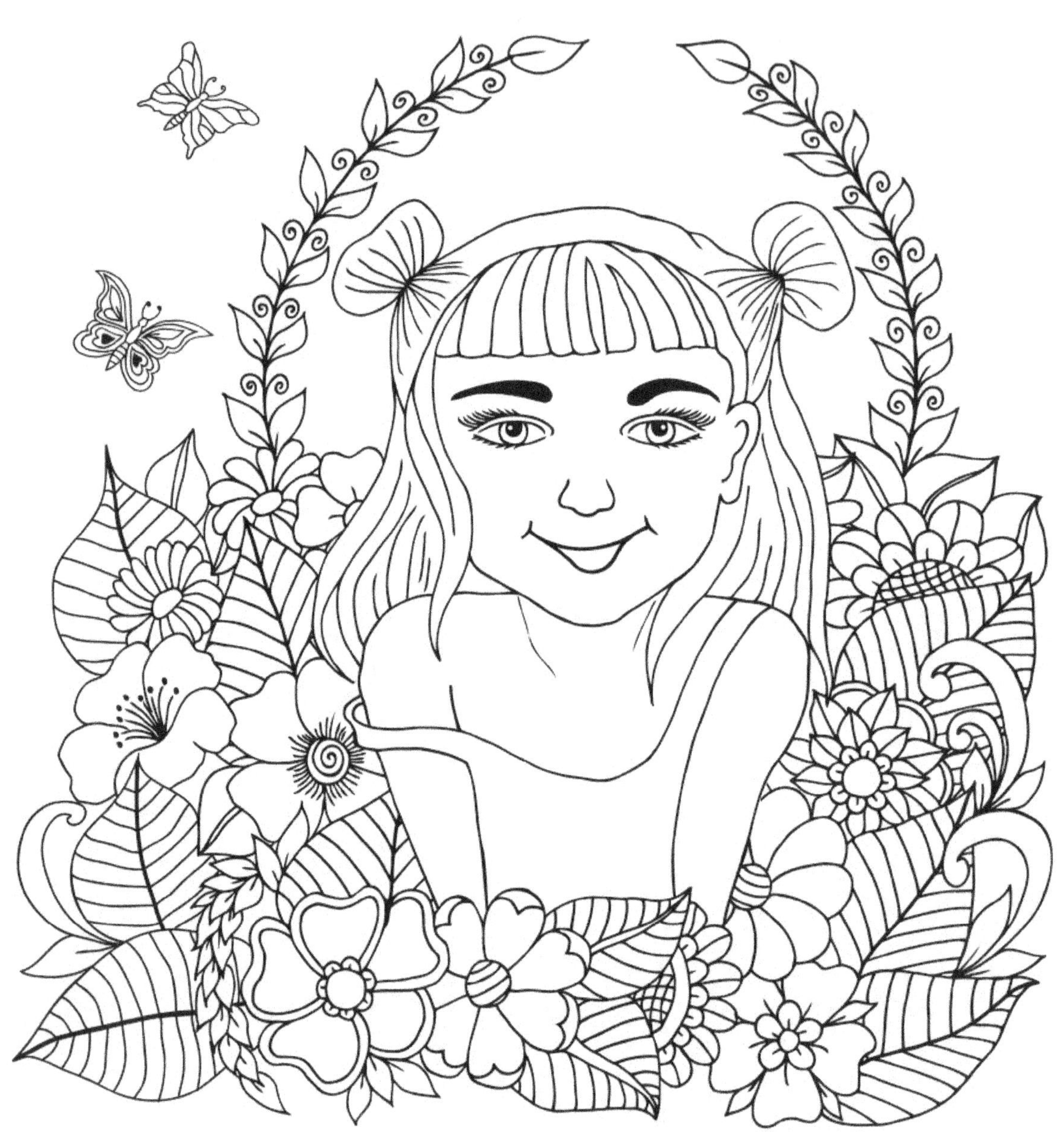

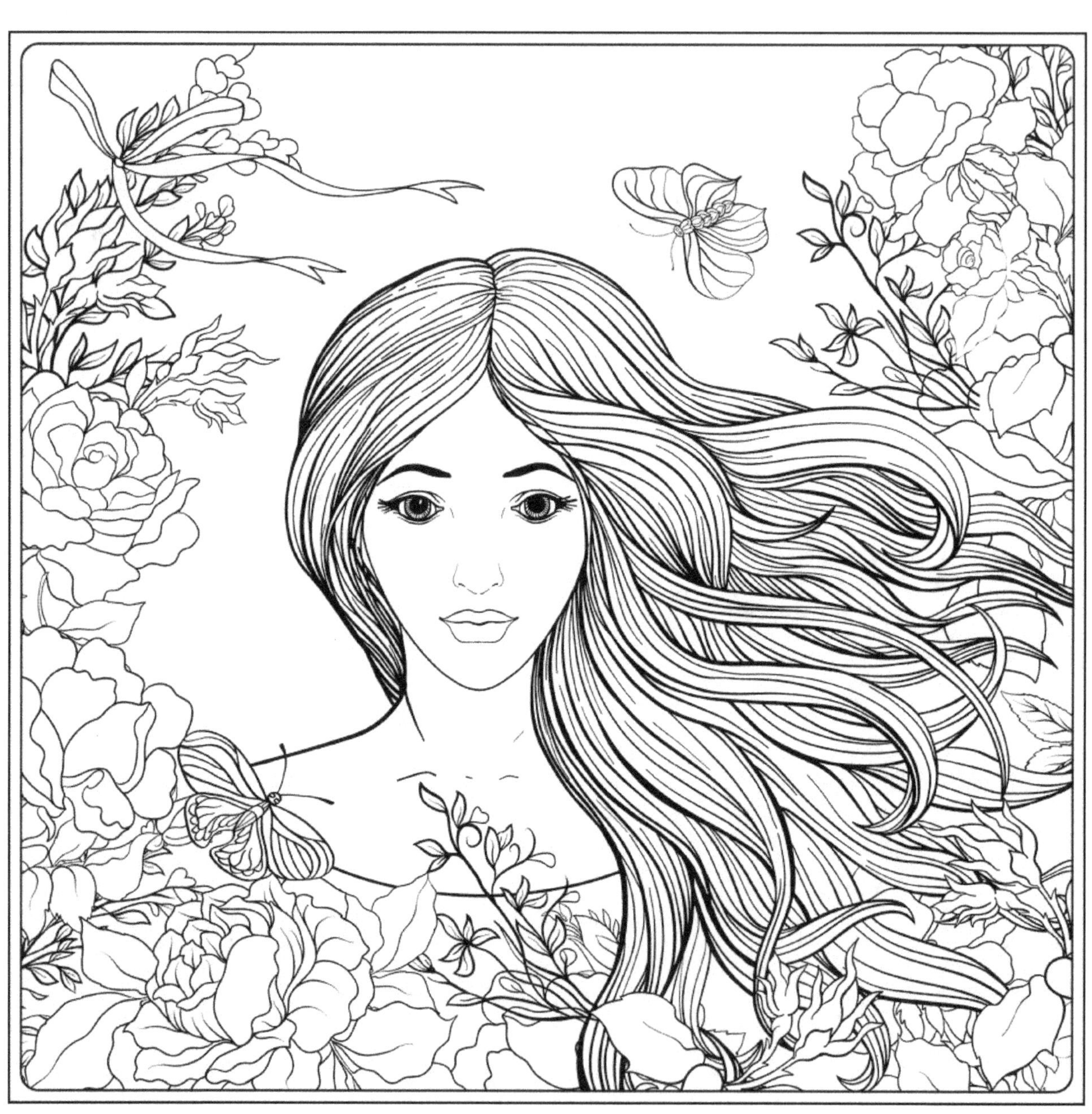

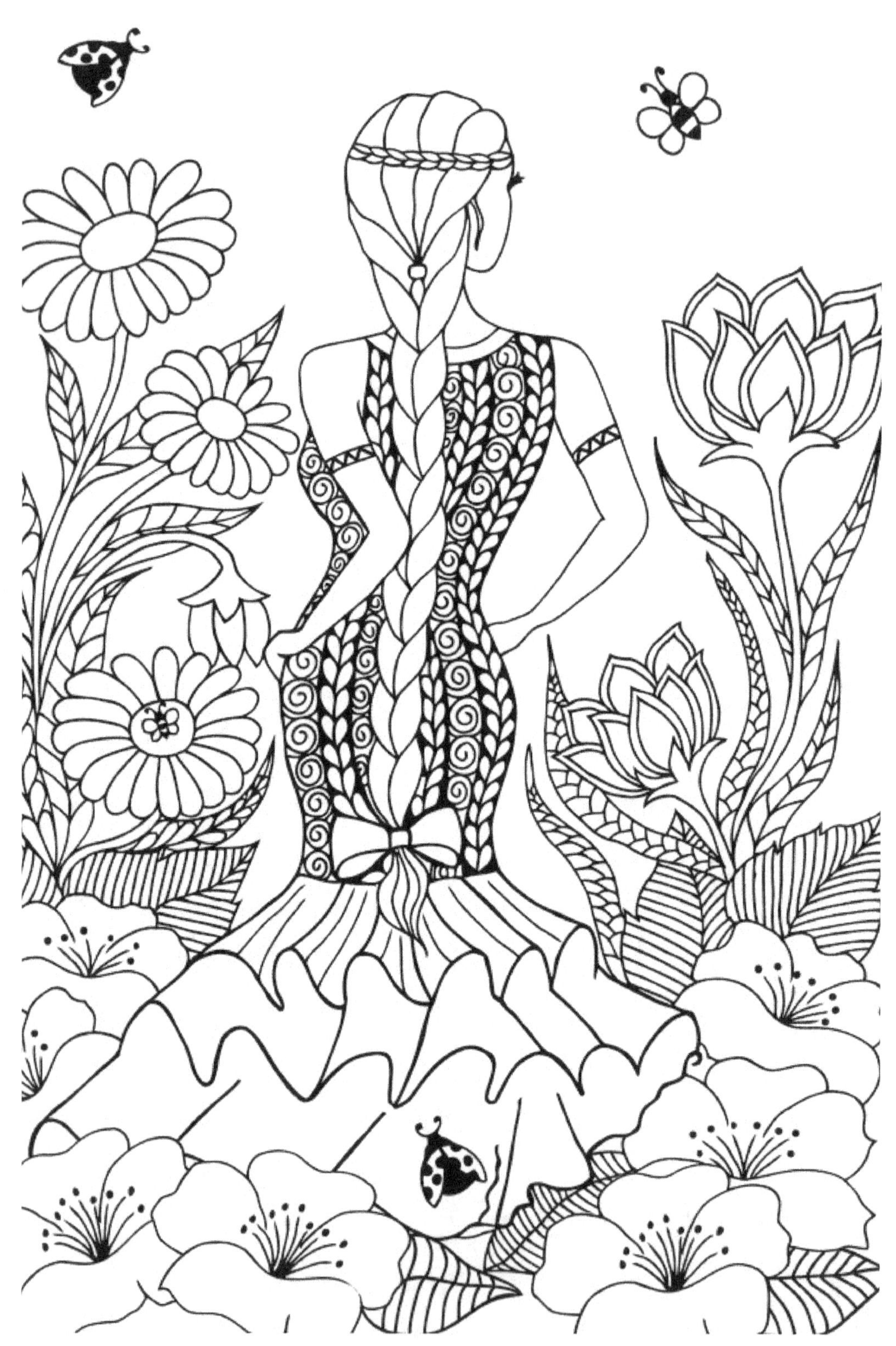

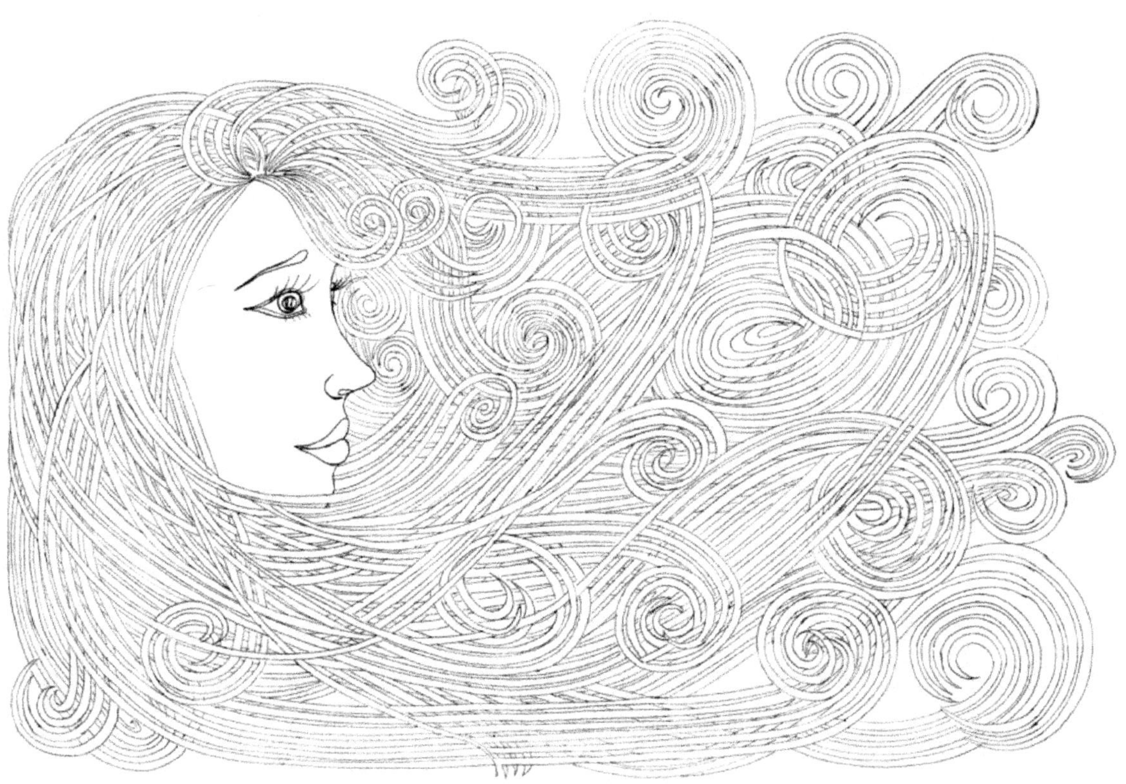

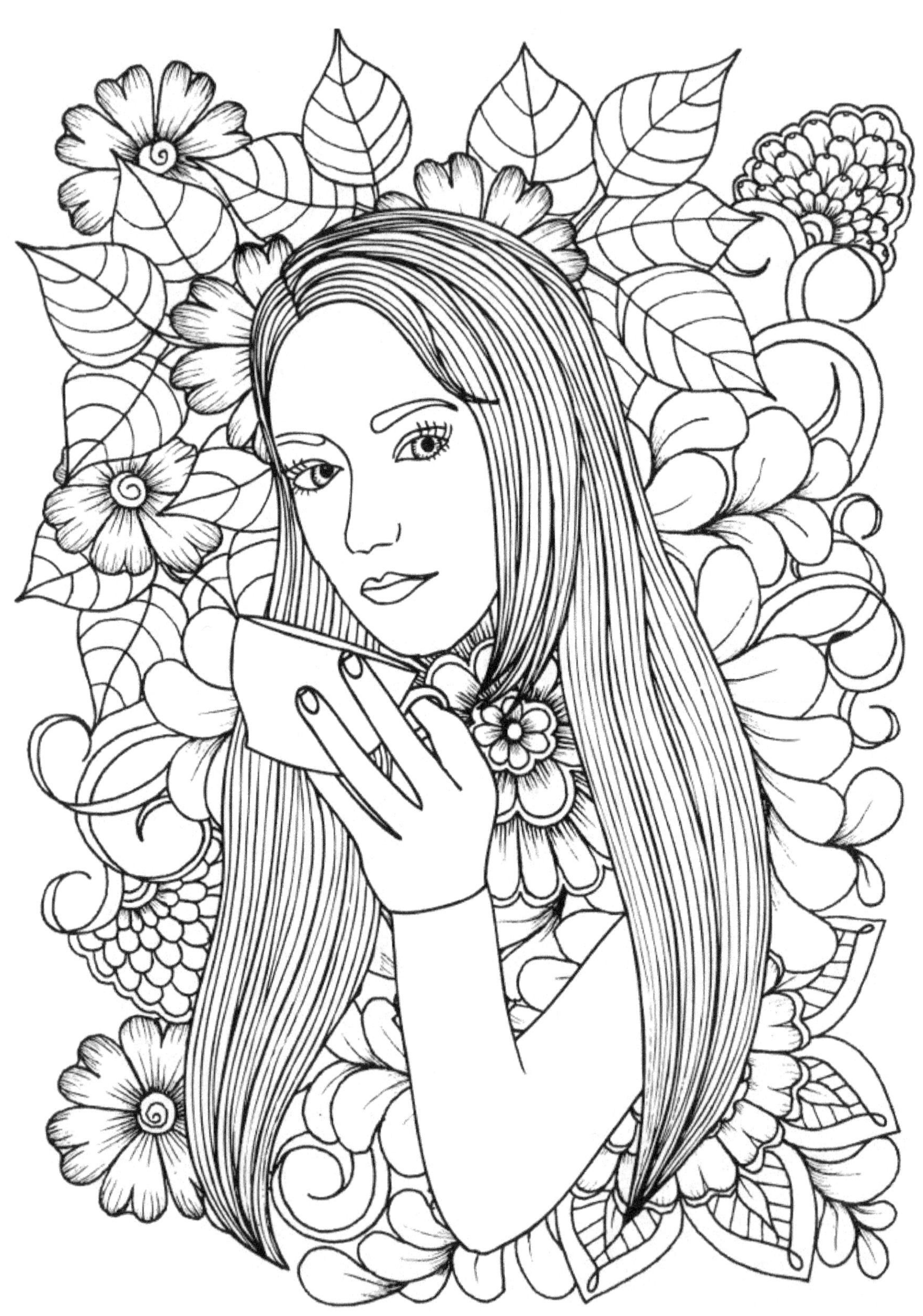

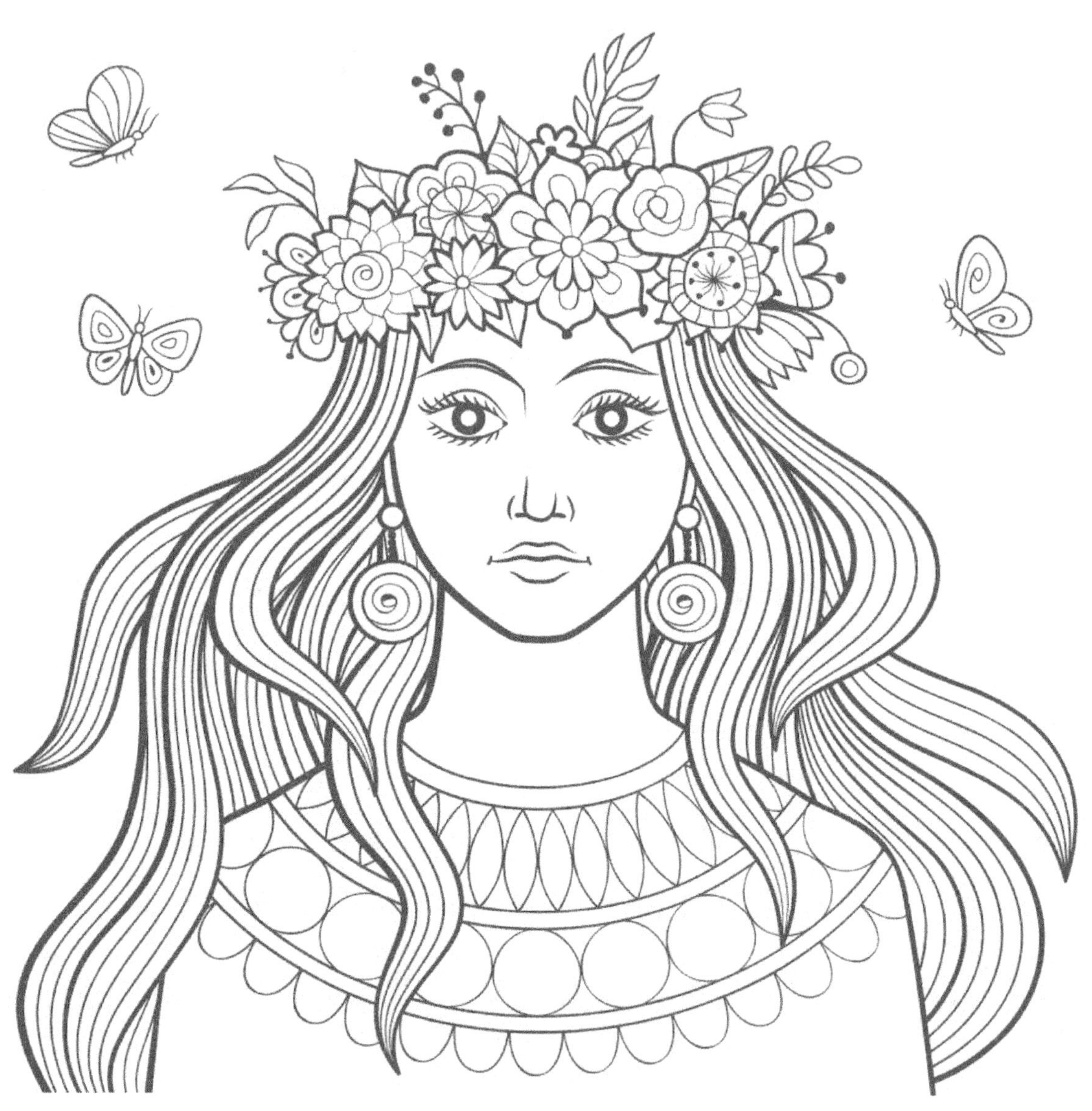

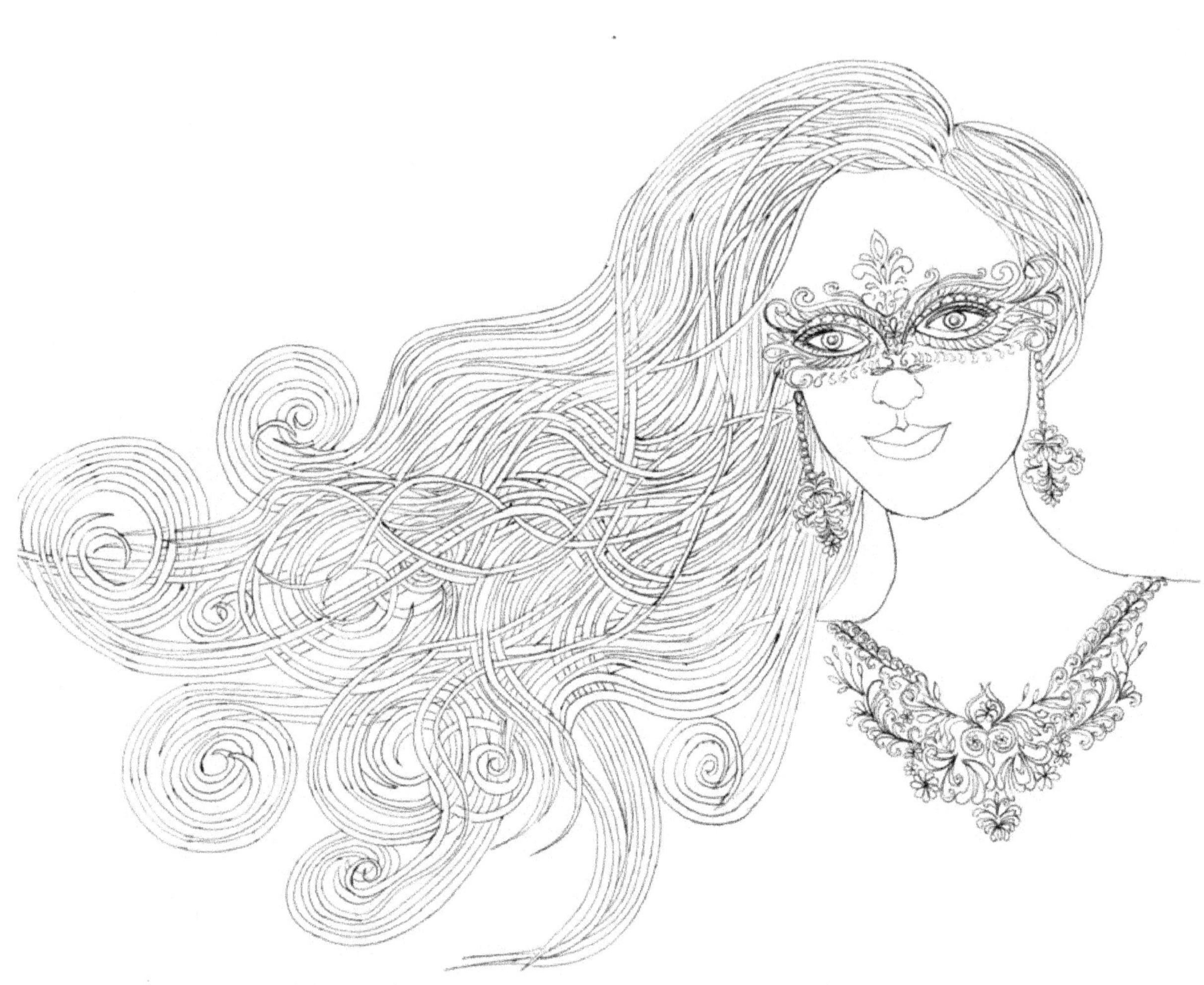

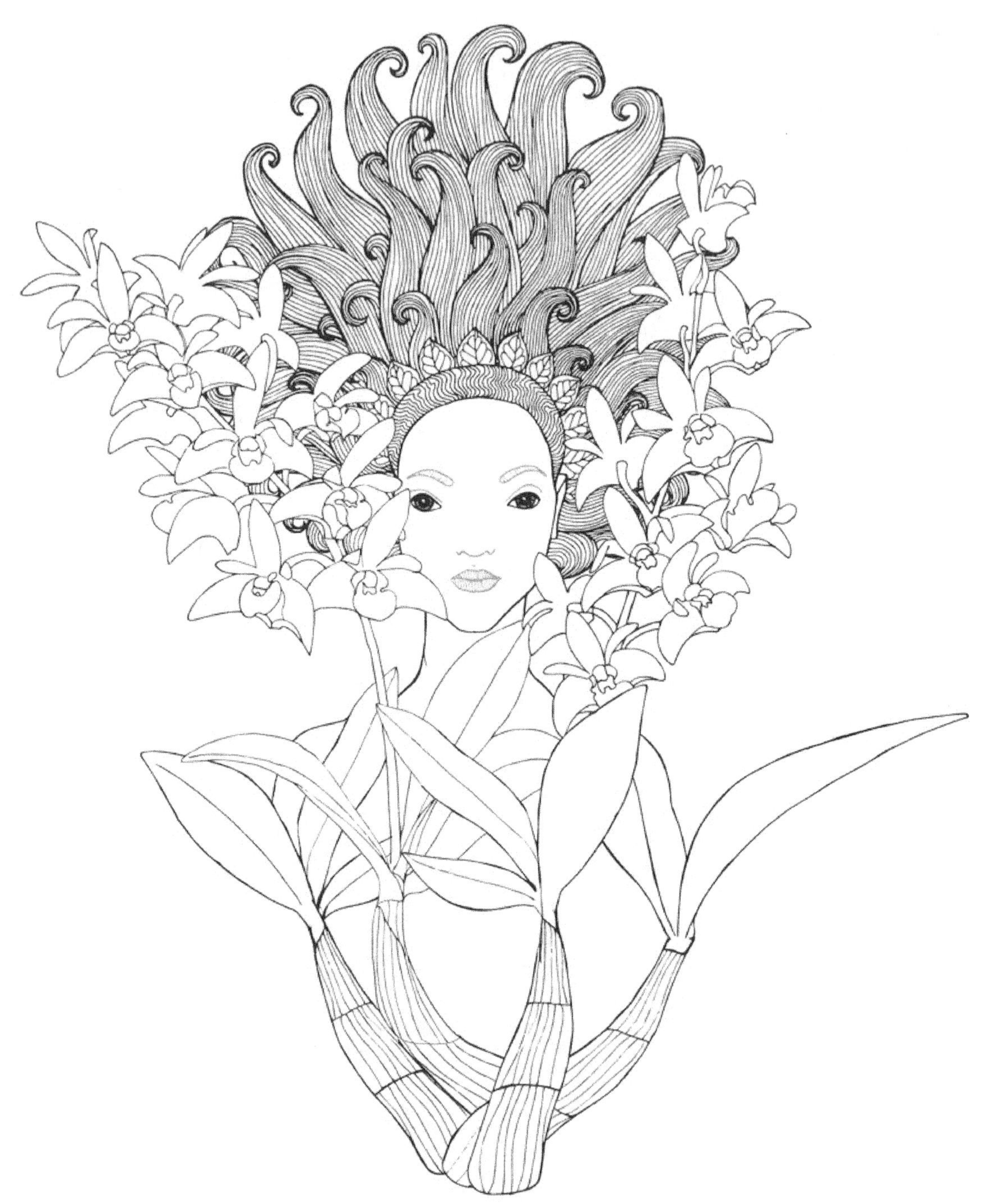

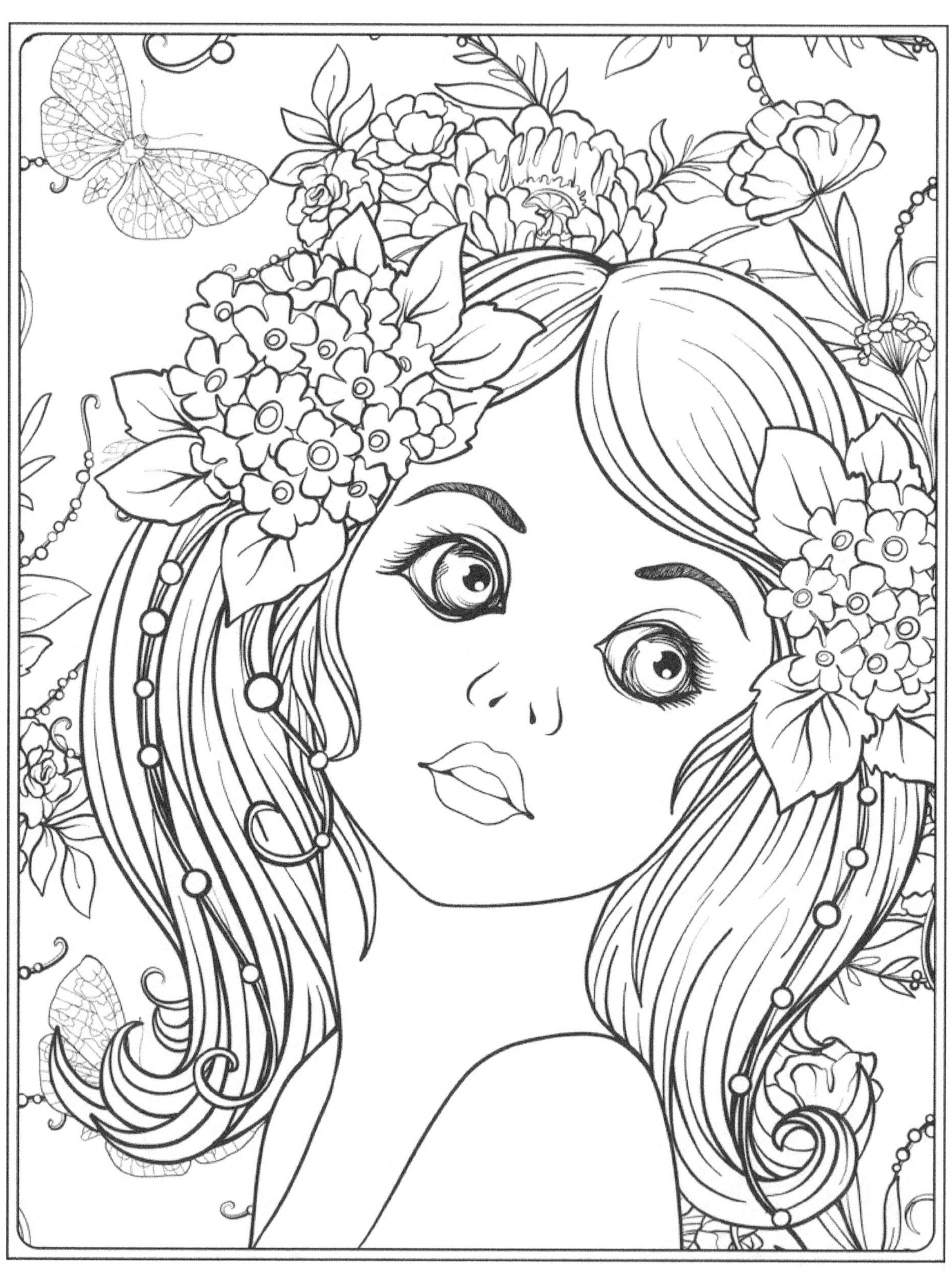

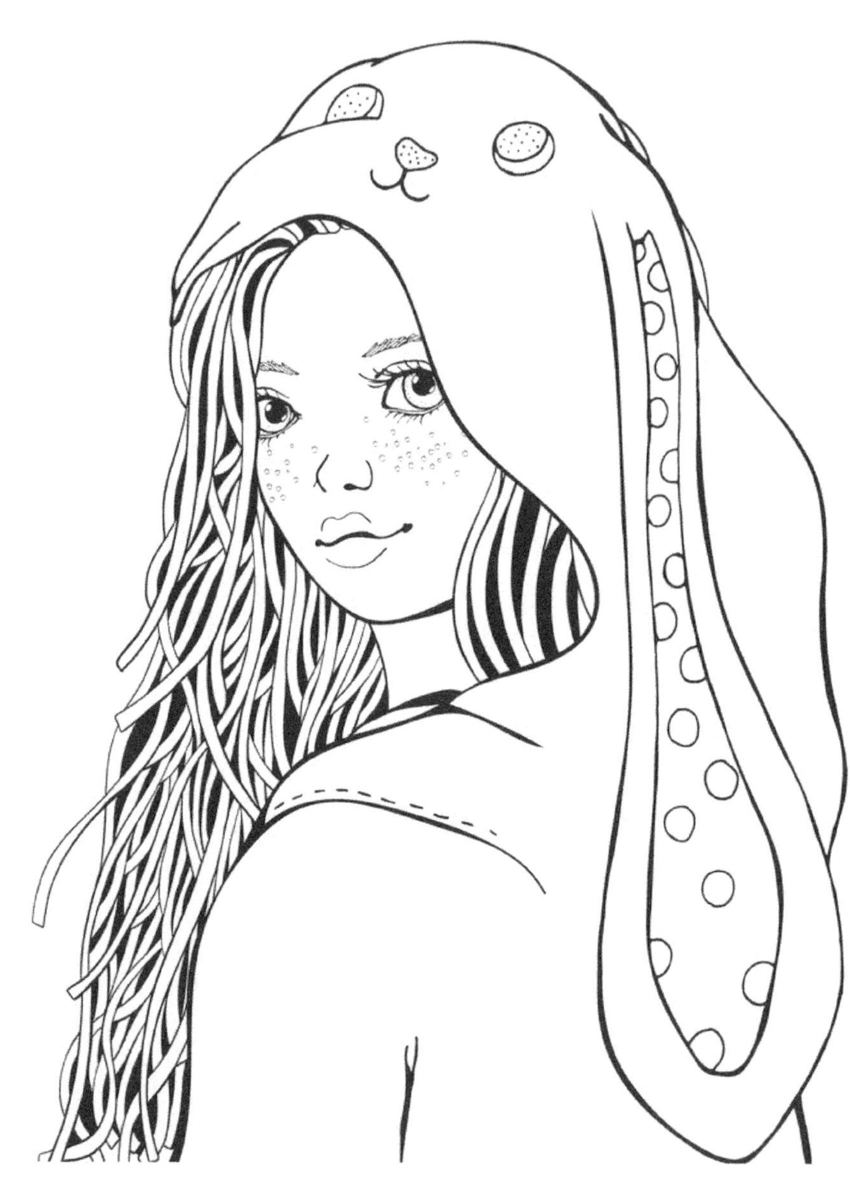

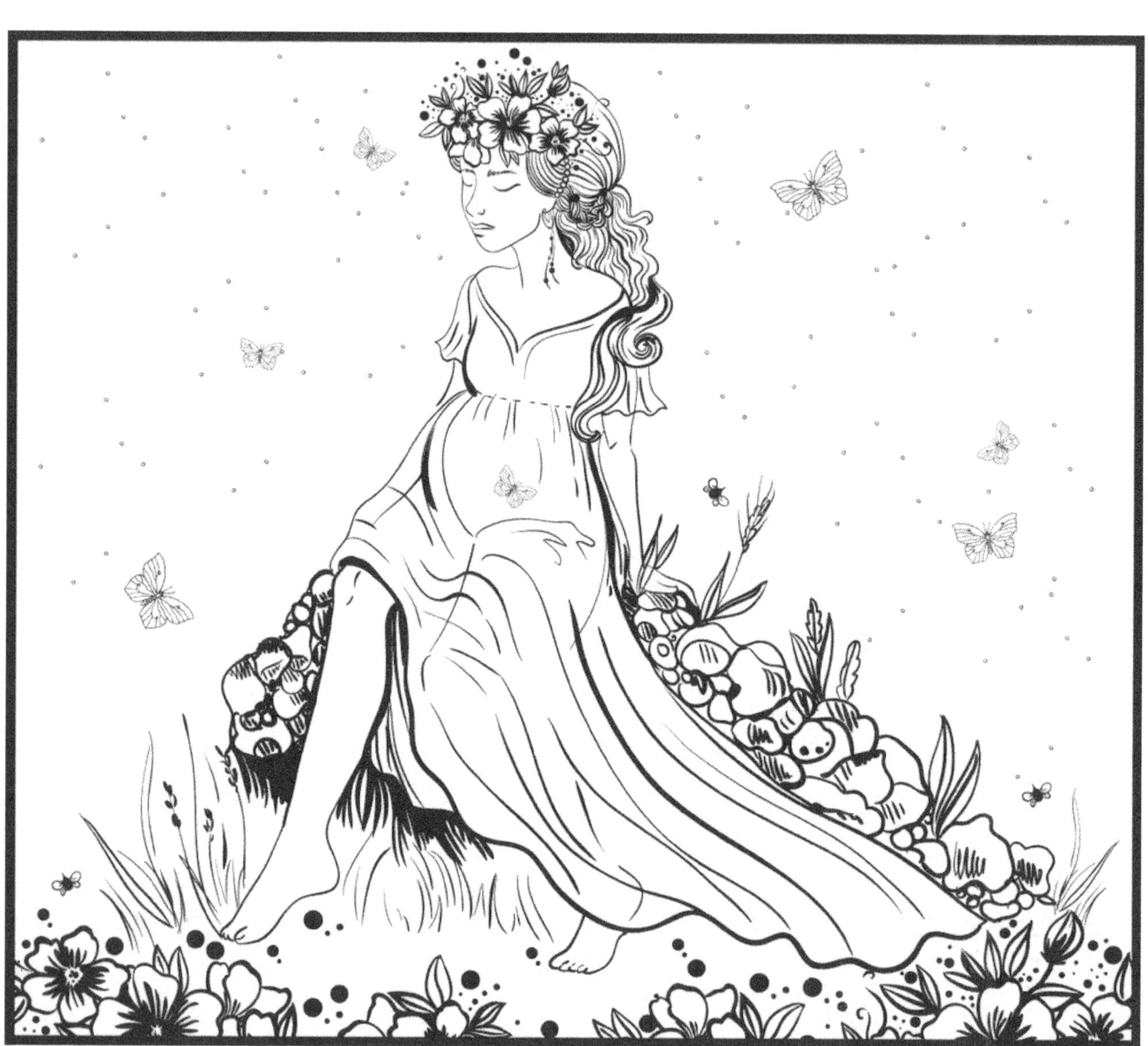

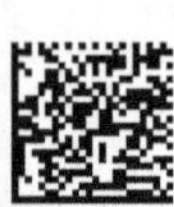